Present Day China

Published in association with
Observer Research Foundation
New Delhi

Observer Research Foundation (ORF) is a public policy think-tank that aims to influence formulation of policies for building a strong and prosperous India. The ORF pursues these goals by providing informed and productive inputs, in-depth research and stimulating discussion. The Foundation is supported in its mission by a cross-section of India's leading public figures, academics and business leaders.

Present Day China

A Net Assessment

ORF CHINA STUDIES SERIES # 5

ACADEMIC FOUNDATION
NEW DELHI

www.academicfoundation.com

First published in 2012
by

ACADEMIC FOUNDATION
4772-73 / 23 Bharat Ram Road, (23 Ansari Road),
Darya Ganj, New Delhi - 110 002 (India).
Phones : 23245001 / 02 / 03 / 04.
Fax : +91-11-23245005.
E-mail : books@academicfoundation.com
www.academicfoundation.com

in association with the
Observer Research Foundation, New Delhi

Cataloging in Publication Data--DK
Courtesy: D.K. Agencies (P) Ltd. <docinfo@dkagencies.com>

Present day China : a net assessment.
p. cm. -- (ORF China studies series ; no. 5)
ISBN 13: 9788171889648
ISBN 10: 8171889646

1. China--Economic conditions--1949- 2. China--Foreign relations--1976- I. Observer Research Foundation. II. Series: ORF China studies series ; no 5.

DDC 330.951 23

Typeset by Italics India, New Delhi.
Printed and bound in India.

Contents

About the Editor/Contributors

Editor:

M. Rasgotra joined the Indian Foreign Service in September 1949. In the pioneering years of Indian diplomacy, he served with distinction in Indian missions in Washington D.C., Kathmandu and in the Ministry of External Affairs. From 1958 to 1962, he was India's representative on the UN Trusteeship Council, the UN General Assembly's Fourth Committee and the Decolonisation Committee. From 1962 to 1967, he made a notable contribution to the evolution and implementation of India's policies towards its neighbours.

Rasgotra's ambassadorial career took him to Morocco and Tunisia, the USA, the UK, Nepal, the Netherlands, France and UNESCO. His tenure as Foreign Secretary from 1982 to 1985 was marked by a renewal in Indo-American relations, sustained negotiations with Pakistan and an opening to China. He played a significant role in the prestigious events of the period—the Seventh Non-Aligned Summit, the Commonwealth Heads of Government Meeting, the Six-Nation Appeal on Nuclear Disarmament and the Six-Nation Summit in New Delhi.

After retirement, he was Honorary Visiting Professor at JNU, Regents' Professor at the University of California, Los Angeles (UCLA), and President of the Delhi College of Arts & Commerce. He is founder President of the International Institute of Asia-Pacific Studies. Currently, he is President, Centre for International Relations at the Observer Research Foundation.

In 2002, he was decorated with the Padma Bhushan.

Contributors:

Madhu Bhalla, is Professor at the Department of East Asian Studies, University of Delhi. Her areas of interest are: China's foreign policy, security policy and political economy. She has participated and presented papers in several national and international conferences.

Vivek Bharati is Executive Director for External Affairs at PepsiCo India. Prior to this, he was advisor for national policy and programmes at Federation of Indian Chambers of Commerce and Industry (FICCI).

Ravi Bhoothalingam studied Experimental Psychology at Cambridge University, UK. After holding senior positions in industry in India and overseas, he now serves on several company boards and travels extensively in China and Mongolia to promote cultural and business ties.

Sreemati Chakrabarti is Professor in the Department of East Asian Studies, University of Delhi and Honorary Fellow of the Institute of Chinese Studies, Centre for the Study of Developing Societies (CSDS), Delhi. She has done her MA in Regional Studies-East Asia from Harvard University and PhD on 'Perceptions of China and Naxalite Ideology' from Columbia University. Her publications include *China and the Naxalites* (1990), *Mao, China's Intellectuals and Cultural Revolution* (1998) and *Introducing China* (1995), as well as numerous articles and research papers on aspects of modern Chinese politics. Currently she is working on China's education.

Ajish P. Joy is Assistant Editor, *The Week*. Prior to this, he worked with Observer Research Foundation (ORF), New Delhi. He completed his PhD from the School of International Relations, Jawaharlal Nehru University, New Delhi. He has published a book, *India, Central Asia and Russia: Potential for Regional Co-operation* (2007). He has also contributed chapters and articles in edited books and journals.

Rajiv Kumar is Secretary General, Federation of Indian Chambers of Commerce and Industry (FICCI). He is a well known economist and the author of several books. Prior to FICCI, he was Director & Chief Executive of the Indian Council for Research on International

Economic Relations (ICRIER). He is also a member of the International Advisory Council of the King Abdullah Petroleum Studies & Research Centre (KAPSARC), Riyadh. Dr Kumar was a member of the National Security Advisory Board (2006-2008) as well as a non-executive Director on the Central Board of the State Bank of India for three years ending September 2011. From 1987-1989, he was a Professor at the Indian Institute of Foreign Trade; subsequently, he worked for the Government of India from 1989 to 1995, first in the Bureau of Industrial Costs and Prices, Ministry of Industry and then as Economic Adviser in the Department of Economic Affairs, Ministry of Finance. In 1995, Dr Kumar joined the Asian Development Bank in Manila and assumed several positions during his 10-year term. In 2004, he joined the Confederation of Indian Industries (CII), New Delhi as Chief Economist. He has a DPhil in Economics from Oxford University and a PhD from Lucknow University. He is a columnist in leading business dailies.

Dilip Lahiri is a Visiting Fellow at Observer Research Foundation (ORF) and a former Indian diplomat, with long and diversified experience in international relations in the Indian Foreign Service. His postings outside India were as Ambassador to France, Spain, Peru and Bolivia; he has worked and toured in many countries in South East and East Asia, the Middle East, Africa, the US and Europe, Central America, the Pacific islands and the Caribbean. He was also Dean of the Indian Diplomatic School. Ambassador Lahiri led the Indian delegation to the Rome conference on the International Criminal Court, was a member of the Indian delegation to the Kyoto Conference on Climate Change, attended several sessions of the UN General Assembly, and has been involved for many years in the negotiations on the restructuring of the UN and expansion of the Security Council, in the UN Human Rights Commission and the Commission on Disarmament. He has spoken at several international seminars and published articles in journals and newspapers on Indian nuclear and security policy, and organised and edited a two-volume compilation on *Indian Foreign Policy: An Agenda for the Twenty First Century* and a Spanish language book of essays by Spanish and Indian experts titled *India and Spain: 2000 Years of Interaction*.

Smita Purushottam is Indian Ambassador to Venezuela. She was Senior Fellow at the Institute of Defence Studies & Analyses (IDSA), New Delhi. She had previously served as Joint Secretary at the Foreign Service Institute of the Ministry of External Affairs (MEA), Joint Secretary in the Integrated Defence Staff Headquarters in the Ministry of Defence; Director/Under Secretary (East Europe/Soviet Union) and SAARC, and Under Secretary (Bhutan) in MEA. She has served in India's missions abroad, as Deputy Chief of Mission in the Embassy of India in Berlin, Minister (Political) at the High Commission of India, London, Counsellor for economic and commercial affairs at the Indian Embassy in Beijing, at the Embassy in Brussels, and the Embassy of India, Moscow. She spent a year as Fellow at Harvard where she prepared a paper 'Can India Overtake China?' (2001).

P.S. Ramakrishnan is a Professor and Indian National Science Academy (INSA) Honorary Senior Scientist at School of Environmental Sciences, Jawaharlal Nehru University, New Delhi. He contributed a paper, 'Coping with Environmental Uncertainties to Climate Change from a Developing Country Socio-ecological System Perspective', to the Report on the Intergovernmental Panel on Climate Change (IPCC) that won the 2007 Noble Peace Prize.

B. Raman is an expert on security and anti-terrorism operations. He is a former Additional Secretary, Cabinet Secretariat, of the Government of India and former head of the counter-terrorism division of India's external intelligence agency Research and Analysis Wing (RAW). He has been a member of various special task forces related to security and intelligence issues. An internationally acclaimed writer and lecturer, he regularly contributes articles to various national and international publications on security-related topics. He is currently the director of the Institute for Topical Studies, Chennai. Raman is also a contributor to the South Asia Analysis Group (SAAG).

Angira Sen Sarma is a Research Fellow at Indian Council of World Affairs (ICWA). Her primary area of research is Central Asia. She has authored a book, *India and Central Asia: Redefining Energy and Trade Links*, and has also contributed chapters in edited volumes. She has presented papers in many national and international conferences/seminars. Before joining ICWA, she worked with Observer Research Foundation (ORF), New Delhi from 2006-2011. She completed her PhD from School of International Studies, Jawaharlal Nehru University, New Delhi.

Nandan Unnikrishnan is a Vice President at ORF's Centre for International Relations. He looks after the US Studies Programme and the Eurasian Studies Programme. An alumni of Jawaharlal Nehru University (JNU), he began his career as a journalist with the Press Trust of India (PTI). His articles, primarily on international affairs, have appeared in many Indian publications. During his tenure at ORF, Nandan has participated in several national and international conferences, lectured in various academic and specialised institutions in India and abroad.

H.H.S. Viswanathan, is a Distinguished Fellow at ORF's Centre for International Relations. He was a member of the Indian Foreign Service and his foreign assignments include Belgium, Zaire, Czechoslovakia, Germany, China, Italy, Cote d' Ivoire, USA and Nigeria. He was the Head of Mission (Ambassador/High Commissioner) in Cote d'Ivoire and Nigeria with concurrent accreditation to Niger, Guinea (Conakry), Sierra Leone, Cameroon, Benin, Chad, Equatorial Guinea and São Tomé and Príncipe. He has been Deputy Secretary (East Europe) and Joint Secretary (Administration) in the Ministry for External Affairs. He represented India in the African Development Bank (AfDB), International Fund for Agricultural Development (IFAD) and Food and Agricultural Organization (FAO). He was also Observer at the Economic Community of West African States (ECOWAS). He has participated in several conferences/seminars/workshops in UC, Berkley, UCLA, Stanford University, CSU, Riverside, Nigerian Institute of International Affairs and University of Sienna (Italy).

Foreword

This book forms part of the Observer Research Foundation's (ORF) ongoing study of all aspects of developments in China, India's great neighbour, its likely future political and social evolution, its economy and how its foreign and security policies affect India and the world.

There are very thorough studies being undertaken in the United States and several countries in Europe and Asia. There is also a certain amount of good work being done on China in some Indian universities, by scholars and former diplomats who have had direct personal experience of China, but all of it put together is far from adequate. To be properly understood, this huge and powerful country, the cradle of an ancient and evolving civilisation, demands a much more sustained and methodical study. We in India need to know China better. ORF's China Studies programme is an effort in that direction.

This volume is an attempt to make an overall assessment of present-day China. The papers examine various aspects including internal political and economic situation, environmental issues, and China's relations with neighbours and major international players.

The ORF encourages freedom of expression of all points of view. And that is the case with this book and our other publications. The authors alone are responsible for the facts sand opinions expressed in their contributions: these do not necessary reflect the views of the ORF.

— M. Rasgotra
President,
ORF Centre for International Relations

Introduction

H.H.S. Viswanathan

How to make an overall assessment of China and predict the future direction based on what it is today, has been the main objective of this publication. The concentration has been to base the arguments on the current status of China in various sectors like internal political situation, internal economic situation, state of science and technology, environmental issues and China's relations with major international players. No country's, least of all China's, future course can be discussed without reference to its history, both ancient and contemporary. Nonetheless, the stress here is to base the projections on the contemporary state of affairs with only minor forays into its past.

A good point of departure or reference, if you will, is the end of the Cold War and the launch of the globalisation process in the beginning of 1990s. China's economy had reached a certain level of maturity in the 12 years of reforms and opening up initiated by Deng Xiaoping in 1978. Yet, nobody could predict the exponential growth of the economy in the next 20 years. How did China manage that growth? Was it only because of globalisation or did China take special initiatives to leverage the process to achieve spectacular results? Can this success be sustained over a long term or are there inevitable barriers to further growth? Has China created for itself new problems and challenges in its quest for the rapid economic growth? If so, will China be able to address these challenges? The overall assessment of these papers seems to present a rather positive picture. Yes, China faces huge challenges. But the leadership seems to be serious in addressing them and putting in place mechanisms and systems to mitigate the adverse effects.

Take the internal economy, for example. With 1990 as base, China has consistently doubled its GDP every five years. This was largely based on the 'FDI and export' model. This has run its course. With the global financial crisis of 2008, and the subsequent slowdown of economies in Europe and North America, the export opportunities came down considerably. China's currency, Renminbi, is also steadily becoming stronger making exports less competitive. The export led growth also caused serious regional imbalances in the development of the country as a whole. The coastal regions progressed at unimaginable rates to the detriment of the hinterland. This has also triggered other problems like urbanisation and unequal growth. Environment is another sector which has been affected very seriously. To address all these issues, China has already started on a course correction. They are now trying a 'rebalancing' of the economy, meaning moving away from export led growth and increasing domestic consumption. Whether the pace of this rebalancing is adequate is a question that is debated in various fora, but a beginning has been made. There are also efforts to shift some manufacturing facilities to poorer interior regions to bring about a more equitable distribution of economic opportunities.

The internal political scene is more complicated. The Chinese Communist Party has been able to keep a firm grip on the situation. Even though democratisation at the grassroot level has been proceeding impressively, a Western style multiparty system is nowhere in sight. Even most of the protests (more than 70,000 in 2010) are of an economic and social nature where citizens are fighting for better wages, better living conditions and amenities. Protests based on ethnic identities, however, are very different in nature and are more serious. Of late, such protests in Tibet and Xinjiang have been increasing both in frequency and intensity. The vulnerability of the Chinese state over these two issues is being increasingly exposed. The situation reiterates the truth that where identity issues have become the main discourse, mere economic development cannot be the solution.

Science and technology (S&T) is an area where China has invested and continues to invest heavily. Even though, China comes way down in the list of Global Technology Index (which is a combination of R&D investment, number of scientific and engineering researchers per capita and the number of registered patents per capita), it is fast catching up with the developed world. They have also begun to build an effective synergy between R&D and the industries.

Analysing China's external relations is an area which needs considerable study in depth. With its growing profile both regionally and internationally, its engagement with the outside world is changing at a rapid pace. The most important question that analysts on China's foreign policy ask is whether China still follows Deng Xiaoping's dictum of 'keeping a low profile' (*taoguangyanghui*) or has it been abandoned. The assertive behaviour of China in the region in the past four years makes people wonder whether China is giving a message that its time has come to be the regional hegemon. This aspect seems to be very pronounced in China's actions towards India and the ASEAN countries. After a careful policy of 'Soft Power Projection' towards ASEAN in the past two decades (China's positive role in the 1997-98 financial crisis in the region is remembered with gratitude), why would China throw away all the goodwill earned by an aggressive behaviour? Is it a prelude to the change of guard coming up in Beijing later in 2012? Or is it a conflict of policies between the People's Liberation Army (PLA) and the foreign policy establishment?

In such discussions, China-US relations attains very special significance. Soon after President Obama took over in 2009, Secretary of State Hillary Clinton remarked that 'US-China relations will be the single most important foreign policy issue for the US.' The relations are much more complex than the traditional ones between a rising power and a declining one. At no point in history have two competing giants been in so much of rivalry and at the same time been so interdependent. There is no historic parallel and hence there is need for careful navigation in managing this engagement. How are the US and China faring in this endeavour? There is still a great 'strategic distrust' between the two powers and despite the increasing interdependence on the economic exchanges, there are fundamental differences on political and strategic issues. Both sides have their own versions of 'exceptionalism' which dictate their attitudes on several global issues.

China's policy towards Europe is highly nuanced as compared to its relations with the US Here again China prefers to deal with the European nations more on a bilateral basis even though there is an institutional arrangement with the EU. Part of the problem lies with the structure of EU itself when it comes to dealing with political issues of importance to

China. On many issues, China is able to take advantage of the differences in the approaches of the major European powers by dangling the carrot of economic benefits that accrue with a positive engagement.

China's role in multilateral fora is becoming more pronounced. It is there on all the global high tables which decide on major international issues. China has greatly benefitted from the current international order. Hence, it would be in no hurry to bring about drastic changes in the order. Nonetheless, its long-term strategy would be to become a 'rule maker' rather than continue as a 'rule taker'. Already, China has started questioning some of the current templates and practices followed in international affairs. China is aware that many developing countries look up to the Chinese model of growth and development with admiration.

All these have profound implications for India. As a neighbour of China who has both unresolved issues with it and at the same time a significant interdependence, India will have to fine-tune her engagement with China constantly. The bottom-line, however, was very succinctly articulated by Foreign Secretary Nirupama Rao in her Keynote Address,[1] when she said that two major factors have to be kept in mind when our bilateral relations with China are discussed: (1) to see India and China only as rivals in various spheres is an over-simplification and an over-generalisation, and (2) the leadership on both sides understand the untenability of any sustained estrangement. India will have to successfully navigate her engagement with China within these parameters.

1. ORF China Seminar Series on *Whither China: Prospects and Direction (Overall Net Assessment of China)*, December 3, 2010, New Delhi.

1 China's Economy

Strengths and Weakness

Rajiv Kumar

China's 'economic miracle' has been breathtaking, historical and unprecedented. A sustained three decade 10 per cent growth has not been recorded anywhere else in human history. It has lifted 400 to 500 million people out of abject poverty. This is something we should all give due credit. In 1978 India's per capita income was higher than that of China's, whereas today we are at about a third, if not a fourth, of China's per capita income. China's record in reduction in poverty has also been exemplary. This is something that we need to bear in mind because we often confuse inequality with poverty. In the public discourse in this country, there is a constant harping on the trade-off between growth and inequality. China has shown that if you can tackle degrading and dehumanising poverty, inequalities do not matter perhaps to the population as much; Chinese inequalities have been rising but because there is no degrading poverty, inequality between Shanghai and Xinxiang or Shanghai and Guangzhou does not really come out as a domestic political problem. It might emerge as a problem in the future, but that is another matter.

China's focus has also been on reducing poverty, and creating mass employment. President Hu Jintao, when asked about three or four years ago about what kept him awake at night, he said it was the prospect of finding jobs for 25 million people. I wish people in our country would also keep awake at night thinking about ways of finding those jobs and forget about everything else. In the early 1990s when I was in the Ministry of Finance I was associated with preparing the annual Economic Survey. I recall that a paragraph was introduced to the effect that it was crucial to provide for full employment and the rest would be taken care of. Let us first get to the situation where we do not have children working in factories and domestic servants being available at less than $50 a month and then we can talk about the rest of the problem.

China is today the second largest economy in the world in nominal terms. It is the largest exporter in the world, and has overtaken Germany. Further, its export structure is changing dramatically: 88 per cent of Chinese exports today are technology items. China hardly exports any primary product except for rare earths, an item which has been in the news lately. Their export surplus is larger than our total export today. We should note also that China's manufacturing sector is changing rapidly. In particular, they are ramping up the technological ladder in no uncertain terms and with great urgency. All joint ventures with China undergo scrutiny on the level of technology that has been brought in by the foreign joint venture partner. The entire manufacturing sector is moving up the technological ladder, as in the other East Asian countries earlier. China is also following that trajectory in services. When we call ourselves a service economy, we forget that China is a large exporter of services than India. True, the share of services in their economy is much lower than ours and their share of manufacturing is much higher; as a result the profile of the services in China, do not show up. Further, China does not publicise its successes in the services sector; they keep telling us you are the service provider for the world, while they keep their light under a bushel, following the example of Deng Xiaoping. They have also done well to combine their strong domestic IT hardware manufacturing sector with software development in a manner in which we have not been able to do. Their growing skills in English, and the continued ramping up of skills in this department has taken the world by surprise including the Japanese who too also attach great importance to English language. The only thing we beat them at is remittances. The Chinese do not have a diaspora which will serve the domestic economy because they are not a labour exporting economy as we are. That is a critical difference and something which we almost pride ourselves. My experiences of being an expatriate suggest that this can be a very disruptive growth model. Thus, with $44 billion remittances that we get annually we tend to think ourselves sometimes as labour processing economy, which accumulates a surplus through this medium. China is not doing that and yet their tourism, their rentals, their interest incomes, their services, IT exports and everything which is 'non merchandise', is larger than ours.

These are significant Chinese strengths that we should take note of, rather than dismiss sometimes with derogatory comments on the unreliability of Chinese statistics. The fact is that those days are gone when one could discount the tendency of Chinese spokesman to include potatoes and wheat (with and without husk), in the computation of their agricultural output.

It is widely recognised now that China is the second largest economy in the world (± 5%). The question is what are their weaknesses. The big weakness at the moment is inequality; as the US saying goes, the hem of the skirt has grown much more rapidly than the rest of the skirt which is the coastline. This was the result of Deng Xiaoping's conscious policy that the head of the dragon would move faster than the rest of the dragon. That is what he had said and that is what happened. So, the entire coastal belt starting from Hainan, Guangzhou, Fujian and Zhengzhou, Shanghai, Shandong and up the Manchurian peninsula has grown much faster than any of the central and western provinces have done. The Gini coefficients show this very clearly and if you add to that some of the other inequality measurements carried out recently, especially asset inequality and education inequality then one finds that the inequality indices are even worse than ours (with the qualifier that in China's case, the difference between income inequality and asset inequality is not as large as is our case. The indication is that our inequalities become much larger because of the 'wealth effect' that we have within the country. One must add that inequality is an issue that China is aware of. The last National People's Congress (NPC) session talked about it and they are now ramping up the growth of infrastructure and facilities in the western and the central provinces.

The second weakness is export dependence. China's net export i.e., export minus import, contributes 105 per cent of GDP; in India's case it is -8 per cent. This is a difference of 18 points. This has to read together with the low share of consumption i.e., 36 per cent on the average. The figure for most economies is about 65-66 per cent. In the case of the US it is 78 per cent or even more. The third weakness is the clear indication of an asset bubble in the Chinese economy. In Shanghai and in the Pearl River Delta there are large complexes of unoccupied housing, including unoccupied official residences. Rapid increases in real estate property is a tiger that they cannot seem to dismount. In terms of their incentive structure through the Party and down to the state and county level, it appears that the best way the Party chieftains can stake their claim to go up the Party hierarchy, is to show how much investment they can pour in, and how many spanking new buildings they have been able to create. Given that incentive structure, it appears that the instructions that emanate from Beijing about tightening of the money and supply are not having the required effect. If the Chinese asset bubble gets pricked, it will create a much messier situation than perhaps the Japanese equivalent. Equally significant is the excess capacity that they have created in several industries and for which they have to find a market abroad and these are mostly intermediates, chemicals, steel, non-ferrous metals and finished products. The last weakness is summed up in the famous statement that the 'Chinese faces the danger of becoming old before they become rich.' This is the consequence of their one child policy, the deleterious consequence of which is that, while it may be good for the rest of the world, in China's case it does mean that they are already facing a rising wage cost and they do not know how to handle it.

Looking at the future, two critical transitions that China has to make today (and which is the defining feature in the book[1] that we did with Raja Menon) are: (i) the transition from external to domestic demand (included within that is the transition from investment to consumption-based demand.) Investment today is 56-57 per cent of China's GDP, and (ii) the technological transition in the sense, that because given their demographic profile, how does China prevent the prediction that they will become old before they become rich, from coming true. This requires that in the next two decades the productivity level in China, already at $4,000 per capita, has to more than double as it were. Their per capita income and growth can only come now from deepening of the technology factor in productivity increases. This can only be achieved if technological capabilities are substantially increased—each individual produces not US $4,000 but US $10,000 worth of value addition. They are in a huge hurry to do this, and given the technology constraints and the technology denial regimes that China is facing, this is a big challenge. In particular, China has to ensure that they acquire technologies which are more frontline and not merely catch-up; they cannot play catch-up anymore, because that catch-up space has been actually exhausted as it were. So, they are now at the production

1. Menon, Raja and Rajiv Kumar (2009). *The Long View from Delhi: To Define the Indian Grand Strategy for Foreign Policy*. New Delhi: Academic Foundation.

frontier and the challenge is to push the frontier forward. Herein lies the big story of the US-Chinese relationship, i.e., how is it going to play out, taking into account that will be premised on the Chinese investment in and quest for technology.

Let me just go back one step in regard to the first problem, i.e., the transition from external to domestic demand. Can the Chinese be successful in this regard? They are very aware of the crucial nature of this task, and they are bringing all their capabilities to bear on it. Nonetheless, the problem is that exporting to organised markets like the US and Europe is a very different ball game, from spending public money in the internal provinces of China, which can be ridden with bureaucracy, corruption, governance problems, etc. So, while you could generate a huge revenue, as well as value addition and expansion by Motorola exporting from Guangdong to the outside world, it is much more difficult to get the same revenue by expanding infrastructure and public housing, education and agriculture, in the western and central provinces. So, the state's ability is going to be stretched, particularly in the absence of a private sector entrepreneurial class. This is also going to be very difficult because within the Communist party leadership, the influence of the Chinese public sector units is incredibly large. Whereas we tax our corporate structure, but as is well documented, China subsidised its big state enterprises. That is why Chinese corporate savings and not household savings have the larger share of China's domestic savings, unlike in our case where household saving are the largest component because we tax our corporate sector to subsidise our household sector. (The French economist Michelle Petis has done significant work on these themes.) The problem is that nobody in the Chinese Communist Party (CCP) is likely to advocate increasing consumption in western China. Further, consider the fact that China today has a current account surplus of 6 per cent of GDP, i.e., about $240 billion. If you want to reduce that from 6 to 2, it is a 4 per cent shift; one can imagine the extra consumption that one would have to generate in western and central provinces. This is going to be extremely difficult despite the enviable ability that the Chinese state has in project implementation and project execution.

Reverting to the technology aspect, the indication is that China will probably have a trade-off with the US, on the basis that they will invest part of their vast reserves, i.e., US $2 trillion plus, (say 10 per cent of the i.e., $200 billion) in the US rust belts and all the empty spaces that US today has in mid-west and the southern states, so as to resuscitate these capacities in these regions to help to produce out of the US rather than produce in China. That will be advantageous to China; especially because they could then strike a bargain for the US to remove the technology denial regime. Some countries have been expecting that the increasing tension between the US and China will lead the US to actually strengthen the technology denial regime. In the event, one might well find a beleaguered democratic administration in the run up to 2012 saying that the trade-off offered by China is a great bargain and if President Obama can sell to this people saying that he has been able to attract a US $100 billion of Chinese investment, not in real estate but in industrial capacity, then the US Congress might be induced to relax the kind of technology regime that they have in place at the moment. This could contribute to helping China implement its own long-term strategy of improving its technology. Indeed. China is already into all these strategic technology areas of aircraft, aircraft carriers, nuclear submarine, material science and nanotechnology. China is wanting to catch up with the US on the technology front because they know that is the key and the only way they can think of themselves as becoming a world power. It is very important for us to find the niches in an expanding bilateral trade and to look for intra-industry trade complementarities. So far our trade is completely unbalanced and this cannot be sustained. Indian industry will not be able to take it any further. So, what we need to find out is what are the sub-sectors, and spaces in their production networks, which are going to be vacated by the Chinese as their wages rise and as they move up the technology ladder. We should not be embarrassed or ashamed about taking those spaces which would otherwise surely go to countries like Vietnam, Cambodia and Bangladesh. Indeed, this is already happening. It appears that our own national model is that we will somehow or the other thaw up the technology ladder, whereas, in fact our resource endowment militates against it. If we follow the strategy suggested above, we would perhaps be able to prevent the strengthening of the G2 (US-China), if we do not, we face the danger of being frozen out.

2 China's Economy

Internal and External

Vivek Bharati

China is already the second largest economy in the world, with an annual GDP of \$5.5 trillion and that this compares roughly with around Rs.1.5 trillion of India (and a projected Rs.14.5 trillion by the end of 2020). We need to be mindful of the fact that at its current rate of growth of about 9-10 per cent, China is already adding one India every three years or less. There are various projections where China has headed: some say that the current rates of growth will be maintained whereas others project a slowing down. Even allowing for a moderation in growth rate, one should take note of forecasts such as that of the World Bank that China would overtake the United States in 2023. This forecast was made 6-8 months ago and it is vastly different from the forecasts that were made just 10 years ago, when China was projected to overtake the US by 2040 or even by 2035. Thus, China has covered extensive ground and has done so fairly rapidly. One has to visualise a \$12-\$15 trillion economy by 2020 and see this from a superpower military capability perspective. If China devote 5 per cent of its GDP spending to defence you are looking at \$600-\$700 billion defence spending on an average every year and that is as good as a superpower gets. So, China is already on the threshold of superpower status.

The indication is that by 2020, we will, to use archaic Cold War terminology, have a balance of terror sooner rather than later. The sixteenth anniversary of the formation of the PRC was celebrated in 2009, and the military parade on that occasion was very instructive and thought provoking. What was shocking was the range of basically homemade weaponry; J10 fighter aircrafts, D31 intercontinental ballistic missile (ICBMs) that can strike anywhere in the United States and can be concealed on the back of a lorry, short range ballistic missiles, cruise missiles, and symbolically the number of soldiers at that parade was smaller than 10 years earlier.

So, that is the 'teeth to tail ratio'. Also relevant is the fact that there is no dependence on Soviet technology in armaments. Some of the technological aspirations that Dr Rajiv Kumar referred to are already being realised. The armament on display was clearly aimed at demonstrating indigeneous technological capability. You might ask what is new in this, considering for example that the Soviet Union did this earlier. The Soviet Union did not have the economic muscle, whereas China has it. I agree with Dr Rajiv Kumar that no other country since the rise of America has made the kind of economic impact that China has globally. Take for example the index that its foreign trade is virtually 70 per cent of its GDP. We are looking at one of the most globalised economies in the world whether measured in terms of foreign trade or capital flows. Further, China's display of military might in 2009 was measured and contextual. It was contextual in the sense that it coincided with the Western world and the other great powers suffering from perhaps the second biggest recession since the Great Depression, and it was during this recession that China had already demonstrated its economic might unlike the Soviet Union, if you reflect, go back to the Cold War. Even during the Cold War, the Western world had suffered many recessions. As the Soviet Union is sometimes used as a reference point, the relevant fact is that it could not exercise the counter-cyclical impact that China had in the recent recession. That is the crucial difference between China and the erstwhile Soviet Union. One should recall the fiscal stimulus or the total stimulus—fiscal and bank lending—that China injected into its economy of $586 billion (14% of China's GDP). This is an unprecedented intervention anywhere in the world in any economy, keeping in mind of size of the GDP. What is also as impressive as the size of the stimulus, is that even after it lost effect and spread itself out i.e., by 2009, the ratio of public debt to GDP was only 17.5 per cent in China, compared to well over 50 per cent in the case of the advanced countries and in the case of India. There was a budget surplus in 2007, which turned into a deficit of only 2.8 per cent in 2009 and this is expected to fall further (the World Bank projection is that it will fall 1.8% this year.) This is in sharp contrast to the huge deficits of the US, Euro and elsewhere. Further, with its US $2.5 trillion foreign exchange reserves, China has not exhausted its capacity to intervene with another stimulus package of a similar size whereas the West has virtually exhausted its capacity to do so. Simultaneously, the size of China's financial sector has also become quite formidable. Four of the 10 largest banks in terms of market cap are Chinese. It has the world's largest insurance companies, Dr Rajiv Kumar has referred to the buying up of assets in the United States. The Chinese Investment Corporation and Sovereign Fund that has been floated actually could be the instrument that they will use and that is worth over $200 billion. That is the initial capitalisation, and the size could be increased as the need increases. That is the instrument they are going to use in the opportunities or dialogue with the US and the opportunities that will arise in relations with the US.

Now, with reference to the theme of this seminar, 'Whither China: Prospects and Direction' i.e., what are the prospects and the fault lines, there have been doomsday scenarios; e.g. the 'coming collapse of China' and there are others who say China will continue with its runaway trajectory. One notes that China has defied doomsday predictions very convincingly over the last so many years. Yet, China undeniably faces some very serious challenges, and some of them are closely intertwined with the politics and nature of the political system. It is not my brief to get into that political discussion, but I would just spell out some of these fault lines.

There are a number of imbalances or fault lines that people are looking at when they look at present-day China. The first is that the extremely high rates of investment, 57 per cent as pointed out earlier, is huge bank lending. Is this creating an asset bubble? This is an important issue which one needs to analyse. A related issue is that with this huge capital intensity and very low levels of consumption, there is an increase in inequalities of various kinds. The first is the level of inequality between the haves and the have-nots. It is not clear to what extent you can use the words 'haves' and 'have-nots' in regard to China, but the fact is that there are people with better incomes and lower incomes. The other inequality is between regions i.e., between the coastal areas and the inland areas. The third inequality is the rural-urban divide or the rural-urban gap. Linked to capital intensity in is investment, the resource intensity of China's economy. This is triggering debate about the huge negative environmental impact, and whether that resources intensity and energy intensity are sustainable, and whether that itself will be China's unravelling. Yet another imbalance is the over-dependence on exports and the insufficient role played by the domestic market. Some have even argued that China may go the Japan way, because some of the features of its economy are similar to Japan's experience i.e., a very high savings rate, high rates of investment, huge excess capacity, falling return on capital, surge in bank lending creating high non-performing loans and a sharp escalation in asset prices. Indeed one hedge fund manager in fact said recently that China is Dubai, a thousand times worse. However, when you examine the data in detail these comparisons do not hold.

For example, one can look at the stock prices. In 1990 when Japan went to a tailspin, the price earning ratio of Nikkei was around 70 and today despite the 70 per cent jump in stock prices over the last one year, the price earning multiple at Shanghai remains well below 30 and this rise also follows, the fall in 2008. In fact, the value as of yesterday of the Shanghai composite of around 2,840 is less than half of its peak value of 6,124 reached on October 16, 2007. For much of this year, the Shanghai composite has remained below its 200 day moving average. India's stock prices in fact have risen much faster, even as the profit growth has been faster.

Now let us look at housing prices. It is a fact that Shanghai and Beijing housing prices have jumped by 50-60 per cent and this is precisely what has prompted some to say that there is a housing bubble. But Shanghai and Beijing are not really representative of the entire country. The Chinese government has a 70-city property index and various organisations use that to look at property prices. During 2009, this index showed an 8 per cent increase in property prices. But this too had followed a fall in prices in 2008. The World Bank Report on the subject says that rise in property prices were contained during June-August, 2010 (China Quarterly Update, November 2010). Since then they have shown a marginal increase, but the government has reacted by increasing the down payment ratio on mortgages which have gone up from 20 to 30 per cent. The housing bubble argument is further weakened by the movement of average home prices relative to average incomes. This is relevant because in the United States, when the home bubble happened, the loans exceeded the value of the house or even the repayment capacity of the borrower in many cases. If one looks at the top 20-30 per cent of population and their average income, because these are the ones who are buying houses, not the bottom 70 per cent, then the average home price ratio is around 4 to 5 which is very close to the ratio in the advanced world and well under the figure of 18 that prevailed in Japan in 1990. However, much more important is the fact that savings play a much greater role in China than debt in home purchases; nearly 25 per cent of all buyers pay cash for homes. On the average, mortgage covers only half of the home price, unlike 100 per cent in many cases in the West. In Japan in fact there were 100- year mortgages, which is unimaginable. You do not see the same kind of frenzy and irrationality in China. The fact is that they are very proactive and are monitoring the market very closely. We do not do this in India. The difference is as follows: down payment requirements by home buyers, i.e., first time buyers was raised from 20 per cent to 30 per cent. Investors are required to pay 40 per cent. So, there is a distinction. For the second time buyers, there is a higher down payment. The government has also imposed a sales tax on homes sold within five years to prevent speculation. Wish we had a similar thing going in India, with savings are playing a much bigger role than debt in the housing market, (one notes that share of real estate loans in bank lending in China is less than 20%, in sharp contrast to over 55% in the US.)

Let us look at the capital intensity argument. Undoubtedly the investment rate in China, (55-56%) is very high. But, this also needs to be situated in the context of the stage of development. In the 1960s and the United States, both during the war period and immediately after it, as well as before and after the Great Depression, their investment rates were extremely high. That is the time when economies invest in infrastructure and in building manufacturing capacity. The US in the earlier 20th century and Japan in the 1960s had very high rates of investment. In India, as our growth rate has jumped over the last 5-7, years there has been a 10 per cent jump in the rate of investment, (and if we were to cover our deficit in infrastructure sectors, the 36-37% rate of investment, it would be as high as the mid-40s). No doubt there is misallocation of resources in China. But this also needs to be looked at in conjunction with the fact that despite the capital intensity and despite the misallocation of resources, China has seen the biggest total factor productivity increase over the last two decades. There is a great deal of guided bank lending through the state owned enterprises and other sources. So, there are large productivity increases which are taking place in that system. Yet, it is likely that China will continue to face overcapacity in certain sectors and this is one problem which needs to be researched and analysed closely.

Let me give you just one example which will define the Chinese economy. Till about 2003-04, China added about 10,000-15,000 MW of power production capacity each year. In the next five years, they ramped it up to 100,000 MW each year, which is unprecedented in human history. This demands matching capacity in equipment and other items. The investments were also made. When you have such capacity additions every year, manufacturing would be looking at export markets. Anil Ambani's contracts for imparting electricity machinery for China are part of that problem that China is facing in overcapacity in its thermal power, etc. This could be widespread and across many other sectors, although power would be unique in the sense that in no sector has there been a ramp up as in the power sector. So, how would you downsize this capacity? What would happen to people who are working in these factories? So, this is a live issue that needs to be analysed and this leads us to the fact that there is a dominant share of state owned enterprises in the Chinese economy. But let us also look at the fact that it has fallen consistently from 70 per cent in the 1990s to around 40 per cent now. They have preferential access to credit, they get variety of concessions and even during the stimulus period, bank lending was directed towards many of these state owned enterprises. In a market economy when you have excess capacity, the market kills it and restructuring happens. How that will unfold in China is not clear.

Another key issue is regional inequality and imbalance in China. When Deng Xiaoping started his reforms, he deliberately started with an unbalanced strategy of growth unlike Mao who tried to have balanced growth. Deng focussed first on the coastal regions where all these special economic zones were supported by public investment and fiscal concessions, and other inputs and till the mid-1990s, these coastal regions grew much faster than the rest of the country. Over the next five years, some equalisation took place. But over the last decade, the internal regions have started growing much faster than the coastal areas. Simultaneously, even while there are 150 million, a 180 million, or even 200 million migrant workers, over the last 7-8 years or a decade, real wages have risen consistently in China by 9 to 10 per cent. What is also happening is industrial action. Unionised action by workers wages are rising in coastal areas, and consequently much of investment is moving inwards. This is also supported by China's policy. They have also given slogans like 'Go West', the 'development of the northwestern provinces', 'centre rising', etc. So, the fiscal concessions in public investment which earlier favoured the coastal regions, are now moving inwards and that is what is helping together with inward moving multinational investments (perhaps not for export markets, but to feed growing domestic demand). All these factors could help (as well as wage increases) to redress the imbalance and demographic transition. Further, for the first time there are figures to show that for the last two years university enrollments are falling. The number of people between the 15 to 29 age group will start declining in 2012 and the migrant worker force will not be as substantial as it used to be. There are some assessments which show that the 40 plus age group do not migrate as easily as the 15 to 29 segment, and further, that this share taken together with increasing growth rates in the central provinces and even towards the western provinces coupled with rising wage rates and the abolition of taxation on agriculture, increased subsidies to the farm sector, and the huge focus on social sector investments such as primary education, health care, the indication is that the share of consumption in national income will rise, also. Consequently, some of the imbalance which the Chinese government is acutely aware of, as reflected in the various pronouncements e.g. 'harmonious development', will also be addressed. How that will play out also needs to be studied.

3 Technology as the Key to Power

What India can Learn from China

Smita Purushottam

Introduction: Importance of Technology in National Power

Many countries are implementing proactive national policies to ensure that they maintain their technological leadership, realising that this is what gives them the underlying advantage in the global competition for power. Thus, Russian President Medvedev has launched several initiatives for the technological upgradation and modernisation of the Russian economy. United States President Obama has time and again emphasised the need for a concerted national effort to retain America's lead in technology, reminding his countrymen in his State of the Union Address on January 25, 2011 that, 'Maintaining our leadership in research and technology is crucial to America's success.'

Meanwhile, China has pursued a focussed policy which will catapult the country from being a technology absorber and integrator to becoming a technology producer. Chinese products are even now competing with western products in export markets, for example in high-speed railways and telecommunications equipment, thus slowly neutralising the only remaining competitive advantage that a Europe facing demographic decline and anticipated labour shortages has retained *vis-à-vis* China—high technology. Europe's only hope is that China will continue to rely on what we call the 'APE' model—i.e., 'assimilate-produce-export'—with technology copied from the West.

While the jury is still out on whether China can attain the level of the United States and the West and become a technology superpower within the next 5 to 10 years, the telltale sign that this is a proximate possibility—is the increasing nervousness displayed by American and western industry when confronted by the spectre of Chinese competition. This is reflected in barriers to Chinese investment and therefore local production by Chinese companies, resistance to Chinese exports via countervailing duties, and lobbying by the Chambers of Commerce of the United States and of Europe against alleged Chinese technology theft. Disputes between China and the EU, and China and the US, and to a certain extent between China and Russia as well, on intellectual property rights infringements, indicate that every country is taking the prospect of China emerging as a competitor in the technological space very seriously. The Americans and the EU have been ranged against China on the issue of non-compliance with WTO obligations, intellectual property rights and over new legislation mandating preferences in Chinese government procurement orders for domestically innovated products.[1] Russians have also complained of China's successful imitation of their advanced weaponry.

The West now sees that its only remaining USP against a growing China is being whittled away through technology 'outflows', reverse engineering and systemic improvements in China's National Innovation System (NIS). China's advances in technology are providing the ballast for the vast and unprecedented expansion of its national power and are finally beginning to bite.

Hence, technology is emerging as a significant battleground between the West and the East. If we want to be counted as a serious strategic player, we would do well to pay heed to the supreme importance that the contenders give to technology.

The principal theme of this paper is to draw lessons from the Chinese experience in order to provide some additional insights for a possible high-tech, high-growth path for India. A brief snapshot of China's strategy in the aviation sector has been undertaken, partly because an examination of the other sectors would take a few more dedicated months, and also because the aviation sector represents one of the most difficult technological frontiers. It is not surprising that despite its efforts, China has not yet achieved autonomous technological capabilities in this sector comparable to those of the advanced economies, as opposed to its successes in telecommunications,

1. See Purushottam (2010a).

high-speed rail and many other areas. Nevertheless, China has come a long way in this quest in just over a decade, and its determination to tackle the nearly insuperable challenges in this sector shows the strength of its ambition and commitment to scale technological heights. This is in stark contrast to India's passivity and the consequent, continued dependence for all its major requirements in defence, machine tools, aviation sector, telecommunications, IT hardware equipment, many home appliances and now even processed foodstuffs, 64 years after Independence, on imports.

A great deal of additional research is required in this area, as insights are based on and derived mainly from secondary sources (even though they have been pondered over many months and years). However these are excellent, renowned and established sources (Justin Yifu Lin,[2] Tai Ming Cheung[3] etc.) whose conclusions one has little reason to question. This is a work in progress and shortcomings can be remedied with more research but the essential conclusions and recommendations do provide adequate material for a national debate on how best to fashion a NIS which can deliver a sound growth strategy for our country in the context of the demands placed on it by a highly competitive international environment.

The Case for Technological Upgradation of the Indian Economy

As implied above, an essential component of comprehensive national power, especially for major countries like India, is technological power. However, India lags far behind countries like South Korea, Israel and now even China. India not only suffers a chronic structural imbalance in its trade with China, but unlike other Asian countries such as Taiwan, Japan and South Korea; it exports mainly raw materials and unfinished products to China.

The Department of Scientific and Industrial Research (DSIR) and the Indian Institute of Foreign Trade (IIFT) estimate that technology exports

---

2. Justin Yifu Lin, Chinese economist and former Chief Economist and Senior Vice President of the World Bank.
3. Tai Ming Cheung, Director of the Institute on Global Conflict and Cooperation (IGCC) at the University of California. He also leads the institute's Study of Technology and Innovation (SITC) project, etc.

constitute only 5 per cent of India's manufactured exports compared to 30 per cent for China and 54 per cent for Malaysia.[4]

India continues to import most of its requirements in high-tech machine tools, telecommunications and IT hardware equipment, civil aerospace and armaments. India imports 70 per cent of its defence requirements despite several decades of attempts to indigenise armaments technologies. In fact, the Government's own audit report estimates the import component of the Dhruv Light Air Helicopter at 90 per cent. This year, India expects to procure, mostly from abroad, US $15 billion worth of armaments, rising to US $50 billion over the next few years.[5] Over the next few years, the total budgetary provision for capital acquisition (defence equipment purchases) is likely to reach US $50 billion as per indications given by Defence Minister Shri A.K. Antony, speaking at Institute of Defence Studies and Analyses (IDSA) on October 27, 2009. India imports over 75 per cent of its requirements of machine tools which are the basic building blocks of industry.

The much touted services sector does not compensate for the shortfalls in India's manufacturing sector. It comprises 55 per cent of GDP, but only 35 per cent of total exports,[6] not even reflecting its weightage in the economy (the industrial base comprises 28.8% of the economy). It thus does not compensate for the growing merchandise export deficit. Moreover, high growth in India's services sector and consumption-led economy translates into gains mostly for foreign manufacturers and education providers. India imports the bulk of its telecommunications equipment and aircraft for its civil aviation sector, and has failed to leverage its capabilities in the railway sector to build high speed rail manufacturing like the Chinese have. Thus, one of the areas in which India was ahead in the 1990s was in the length of the railway network and also in manufacturing capabilities. But India did not aggressively leverage these assets to generate its own world-class railway manufacturing technology the way China has done. Today China's railway network is growing at a frenetic pace due to massive investments and is planned to expand to 100,000 kilometres. Even more important is the fact,

---

4. *Compendium on Technology Exports*, January 2010, *http://www.dsir.gov.in/reports/iitp_iift/compendium2010.pdf*

5. India apparently imports 70 per cent of its defence needs.

6. Planning Commission (2011).

that China is the world leader in the development of high-speed tracks with 6,920 kilometres ('for trains running at 200 to 350 km per hour'[7]). The aim is to connect the coastal areas to the western interior and hinterland which will contribute to high economic growth in the western parts of China. China also purports to have around 946 patents on high-speed railways and is beginning to export this technology and railway equipment to other countries. There is a huge strategic significance to these developments, as China aims to interconnect the Eurasian continent through high-speed rail networks. The Germans, French and the Japanese are quite upset as China may have 'borrowed' their technology and reverse engineered it to produce competitive clones of their products. India has even finalised a contract to import power equipment from China, a sector in which India has proven capabilities.

And despite laudable achievements in IT, India has not reached the 'controlling heights' in the services sector except in the health care sector. Indian companies have yet to develop their own branded and iconic products in the information technology sector. India's tourism sector lags behind those of other countries and India has not been able to leverage its expertise and skills in the banking and finance sector to create a global financial hub at an attractive location in India, despite aspirations to do so. India's elite is forced to send its children abroad for quality education because of a dearth of high quality educational institutions, and it also satisfies its cravings for light consumer goods substantially through imports. No wonder a senior Officer has quipped: 'India is not even a "banana" republic, it is a *khareedna* republic' (*banana* in Hindi means to make, *khareedna*, to buy).

India's high growth rates of well over 8 per cent over the last five fiscals have thus concealed a growing merchandise trade deficit, projected at an unsustainable 12-13 per cent of GDP by 2014 by the Ministry of Commerce, which makes the following points:[8]

- Import growth regularly outpaces export growth.
- The balance of trade (BoT) deficit on merchandise account will increase to US $278 billion reaching nearly 13 per cent of GDP in 2013-14.

---

7. Dingding (2010).
8. GoI (2011).

- 'This is cause for serious concern because it can lead to an unsustainable current account deficit' (emphasis added).

In contrast, China has piled up US $3 trillion in forex reserves as a result of its export success: exports in 2010 were US $1.578 trillion and imports were US $1.4 trillion leaving a surplus of US $183 billion.[9] In super computers, telecommunications, high-speed rail equipment and technology, which China is exporting to even advanced markets, and some other sectors China has made enormous strides. It would be useful to examine at least one sector to learn some lessons on how China has started producing so many high-tech items across a range of sectors,[10] not to speak of the spectacular advances in the defence production sector.

Chinese Civilian Aircraft Industry, the Civil-Military Integration Model and Mandatory Technology Transfers

How did China achieve its successes? There is no debating that China first created a dynamic economy based on manufacturing and foreign investment. It simultaneously paid a lot of attention to systemic issues—government and state owned sector overhaul and re-engineering, encouraging its firms and R&D establishments to compete in the market and shoulder more of the expenditure on R&D, its educational system, reforms in its patent system, etc.[11] Having a government composed of engineers and technocrats in its top echelons also helped focus priorities on the crucial manufacturing sector. Many assessments of the dynamics of technological development in China have additionally emphasised the role the civil-military integration model (CMI) of development played in creating synergies between the defence and civilian sectors and helping in the two-way flow of technology, especially foreign technologies available only to the civilian sector but usable in the military production sector because of the dual-use nature of these technologies.

In this connection it would be useful to examine the case of the Chinese civilian aircraft industry. Two excellent studies on this subject

9. *http://www.uschina.org/statistics/tradetable.html*
10. China's supercomputer Tianhe-1A was reported to be faster than American supercomputers. Even though they used some imported parts, many components were designed in China.
11. Purushottam (2010b).

are by Andrea Goldstein (2005) and by Cliff *et al.* (2011). China has invested enormous resources, time and energy to overcome the significant entry barriers in this high cost and high R&D intensive industry. It has pursued a focussed policy, directed to establishing itself as a civilian aircraft manufacturer. For several reasons—the Chinese government considers this a strategic industry: China's own market for domestic aircraft is booming and so is the world market, and ascendancy in the civil aviation field—one of the toughest technological challenges—would symbolise China's arrival amidst the group of advanced technological powers.

Civil-Military Integration (CMI) Model

But even more crucially, the technologies for the aerospace sector are closely related to technologies required in the military aircraft production sector. Technologies obtained via the civil route which are otherwise embargoed for China, can and do benefit the military sector. That is also why China emphasises the civil military integration paradigm in its drive to become a technology superpower, as creation of a dual-use economic infrastructure facilitates the two-way diffusion of technology between its military and civil sector.

The Rand report (Cliff *et al.*, 2001) lists the major sub-contracts and joint ventures entered into between Chinese and western aviation firms, as part of the conditionalities mandated by China for access to its market. It concludes—'encouraging foreign involvement in China's aviation manufacturing industry...aids the development of China's military aerospace industry" since "Many aviation technologies are inherently dual-use".' Significant areas of overlap listed by the report are 'computer-aided design and computer-aided manufacturing technologies, precision machining, composite materials, high-bypass turbofan engines, flight-control systems, space launch vehicles, communications satellites, and imagery satellites'. The report lists other collaborations with foreign partners which have directly benefitted the military sector.

The 2009 Pentagon report[12] also has the same assessment: 'China's commercial aircraft industry has imported high-precision and technologically

---

12. *Military Power of the People's Republic of China, 2009*. A Report to Congress Pursuant to the National Defense Authorisation Act, Fiscal Year 2000, at *http://www.defenselink.mil/pubs/pdfs/China_Military_Power_Report.pdf*

advanced machine tools, electronics, and other components that can also be used in the production of military aircraft.'

Mandatory Technology Transfers of Different Kinds

China has aggressively leveraged access to the booming Chinese market to extract commitments for technology transfer, used offsets to kickstart domestic production and assembly of aircraft, compelled foreign aircraft manufacturers to conclude joint ventures with Chinese counterparts as conditions for purchases of their aircraft ('Every C919 contract awarded to a foreign bidder has been awarded to a joint-venture entity'—Rand Report), and played aerospace firms against each other to get the best deals, including those for technology transfer.

Regarding competition between Boeing and Airbus to access China's aviation market, the Rand report cites 'a correlation between major aircraft sales and local subcontracting.' Thus, Boeing lost its, 'commanding lead over Airbus in the Chinese market, accounting for roughly 60% of the Chinese commercial fleet and more than 80% of all new orders' in 1995 'while Airbus held a mere 7% market share. By 2010, however, Airbus's market share had risen to over 43%, while Boeing's share had fallen to roughly 55%...the key appears to be an aggressive and successful program of local production in the Chinese market.' Thus, Airbus may have bested Boeing by agreeing to establish its facility for assembling the A320s in Tianjin.

The Rand report states that 'most major Western commercial aircraft manufacturers and aviation subsystems suppliers have established joint ventures in China', which facilitates 'technology transfers of a more military character', and that the 'technology level of Western aerospace joint ventures in China has increased steadily over time.' The following big-ticket western firms are present in China, several of them having established more than one joint venture: Boeing, Airbus, Embraer, GE, Honeywell Aerospace, Pratt & Whitney, Rolls-Royce, Sikorsky Aircraft Corporation, and a host of other firms. They cover production or development of a mind boggling array of high-tech products and some of them have set up R&D and multimillion dollar training centres imparting training to thousands of Chinese technicians free of cost. Major areas for technology transfer seem to be aircraft engine technology, components, composite-materials, avionics, all kinds of sophisticated engineering and electronic products etc. They have also forged research collaborations with Chinese universities and research institutions, with People's Daily (2010) reporting a US $7.5 million joint research centre with Tsinghua University established by Boeing 'to develop aircraft cabin environments, advanced materials, computer science and industrial designs.'

Assessment

While China has made serious progress in the aeronautics sector, it has a long way to go. The Rand study has concluded that most of the key sub-systems of the Chinese aircraft continue to be produced by established western manufacturers, and is not sanguine about China being as yet able to compete with them, particularly in the large jet sector. Moreover, since 'Western companies have a vested interest in maintaining control of their core intellectual property'—and China has not yet demonstrated the capacity to innovate new platforms—China 'still lags behind the state of the art in virtually all areas.'

This means also that reliance on joint ventures and partnerships with foreign firms is not a sure–fire way to ensure technological transfers of the highest quality, even though China has done much better than India in this department. The verdict on foreign direct investment (FDI) as a conduit for desired technologies to developing markets is at best a mixed one. A recent study on the relationship between manufacturing FDI inflows and expansion of the technological and managerial technological capabilities of Chinese firms by the Peterson Institute for International Economics (Moran, 2011) concludes that there have been very few spillovers between the two. This may account for the situation as it stands in China's aviation sector.

While we keep this qualities in mind, we must also note China has managed to extract relatively more value from FDI in this sector because of mandatory technology transfer provisions in its contracts than it would otherwise have. China has also managed to develop a huge manufacturing infrastructure which has civilian/military components and interfaces (Cox Committee Report)[13] and nurtured a sophisticated supply chain. A viable

13. The Report of the United States House of Representatives Select Committee on U.S. National Security and Military/Commercial Concerns with the People's Republic of China, May 1999.

aerospace production sector has thus been established in China, even though it is not as state of the art as its western competitors.

China has also become part of the global 'supply chains of the world's leading aerospace firms.'[14] Synergies have been established with nearly all western aircraft firms (Airbus, Boeing, General Electric (GE), Honeywell, Pratt & Whitney, Rolls-Royce and many others)—with western firms supplying a significant portion of Chinese aircraft firms' requirements and vice versa. China Daily (2002) claimed that 25 per cent of Boeing or Airbus plane parts are made in China. During his visit to China (November, 2009), the Pasztor and Shirouzu (2009) reported that President Barack Obama pledged to promote greater collaboration and even US safety certification for the ARJ21. An interested party could be GE, which provides the engine for the ARJ21 and hopes to supply the C919. This demonstrates the synergy being established between US and Chinese high-tech industries.

China is now producing the medium passenger jet—the ARJ21, *albeit* major sub-systems are still subcontracted to western manufacturers as noted above. China has also launched the 160-seater jet aircraft C919 which has been positioned as a competitor to Airbus and Boeing aircraft of the same capacity.

Moreover, the Rand report was written before some important new initiatives were taken by China in recent months to accelerate its acquisition of key technologies; hence, it may be too early to conclude that China will not achieve its goals in the near future. China has launched a drive to acquire high-tech companies abroad as a means of accessing and controlling their technologies. Among such targets reported by international assessment sources, including Jane's and Deloitte—are European companies like Fischer Advanced Composite Components (in 2009), Latécoère, a European aerospace company, the US firms, Continental Motors, an aeroengine component manufacturer and Cirrus, an aerospace firm. Page (2011) reported that Aviation Industries Corporation of China (AVIC) partnered with the US Aerospace Inc. to bid for US defence contracts. Jane said these acquisitions could 'enable AVIC to fulfill a number of objectives enshrined in Chinese defence industry reforms, which promote expansion in dual-use and commercial technologies and their adaption for military purposes.'

14. Cliff *et al.* (2011).

China is also contemplating 'increasing foreign direct investment (FDI) in defence-related high-technology sectors' according to Grevatt (2011). Qingfen (2011) reported 'China will "open wider" to the world by encouraging foreign companies to invest, for the first time, in certain industries under a new draft regulating foreign investment, experts said. The select industries, in the recently released Foreign Direct Investment Industry Guidelines, include high-tech, clean energy, aerospace and aviation, new materials, high-end manufacturing and advanced logistics. The guidelines will replace the previous version, published in 2007. There are also changes in the services sector with vocational education and training encouraged in the guidelines and the medical professions are no longer excluded.' Perhaps China is taking a leaf from India's book: India permits FDI in the defence sector, capped at 26 per cent.

Overall, though the verdict is mixed, the civil aviation sector is one of the most difficult of all and sufficient time has not elapsed for China to have attained its goals and meanwhile, China has made commendable progress through its focussed and flexible single-minded policies.

A Digression on the Chinese CMI Model: A Factor for China Pulling Ahead in Economic Growth and Technology

Seeing the relative backwardness of his country after decades of central planning, Deng Xiaoping implemented economic reforms and launched a massive defence economy conversion programme, forcing defence enterprises into the market and mandating that they increase production of civilian goods. But the initial phases of the reforms encountered many problems because of lack of experience. Prof. Tai Ming Cheung (2009) states:

> The restructuring of the defence economy was considered essential to the overall reform effort... A central goal of the reconfiguration was to establish a combined dual use base in which military and civilian activities could take place side by side in the same factories and research institutes.

According to Prof Cheung, the defence conversion process broke down the barriers between the defence and civilian sectors and facilitated the more scientifically directed CMI initiative which followed later. Thus, following the period of strong economic growth, the Chinese, observing the examples of the US and perhaps some other advanced economies, had realised that a sophisticated defence technological infrastructure could not be built by firewalling defence production from the civilian economy. Also, it was clear that while the civilian economy was constantly forced to upgrade in order to remain competitive, the defence economy with its long gestation periods remained relatively static and now trailed the civilian sectors. Part of their strategy was therefore to build linkages between their civil and military sectors and achieve civil-military integration (CMI). An evolved version of Deng Xiaoping's 1978 pronouncement 'the 16-character policy' became the leitmotif for CMI. The 16 characters directed to the forging of an integrated dual-use system, in particular, the establishment of a civilian sector that had the capabilities to meet the technological requirements of the defence sector. The Chinese understood the linkage between a healthy and technologically advanced civilian sector and a modern military sector well. The exhortation in their 16-character policy—'Let the civil support the military'—seemed to indicate their realisation that only a healthy economy could sustain continuous increases in national/military power.

Also according to Prof Cheung, the Chinese indigenisation drive in the second phase of CMI seems to have depended more on 'spin on' than 'spin off' effects, which could imply that the civilian economy contributed to the technological modernisation and increasing sophistication of the defence infrastructure.

These intuitive breakthroughs were systematically brought together in various Government edicts and high-level speeches. The Guidelines for the Medium- and Long-Term National Science and Technology [S&T] Development Programme (2006-2020) by PRC [People's Republic of China] State Council exhorted CMI in several paragraphs. These provided the institutional sanction for civilian-military tech transfers. The Pentagon explained that 'China's defense industry has benefited from integration with China's rapidly expanding civilian economy and science and technology sector, particularly elements that have access to foreign technology. Progress within individual defense sectors appears to be linked to the relative integration of each—through China's civilian economy—into the global production and research and development (R&D) chain.'[15] It adds that

15. Office of the Secretary of Defence (2009).

in contrast, enterprises 'with limited or no counterparts in the PRC civil-industrial sector—have experienced slower progress.'

According to Hsiao (2011), China 'plans to accelerate defense industry reforms in the next Five Year Plan (FYP)', including deepening CMI and an announcement to this effect was made on 'December 30, 2010 at the 2011 Science, Technology and Industry for National Defense Working Committee meeting held in Beijing', by 'Ministry of Industry and Information Technology (MIIT) vice minister, State Administration for Science, Technology and Industry for National Defense (SASTIND) Director Chen Qiufa'. Apparently the Global Times also reported 'that China plans to complete shareholding reforms of its military industries within three to five years—before the end of the 12th FYP—in order to accelerate the process of integrating with civilian businesses and to raise more funds from capital markets (Global Times, January 7).'

The importance of a diversified manufacturing base and the policies to promote it in spurring innovation cannot be overemphasised. There is substantial anecdotal evidence to show that the Chinese at all levels are driving incremental innovation in a host of sectors, driven by the laws of competitive advantage suggested by Michael Porter in his seminal work.[16]

China has also Aggressively Copied Technology

There is no doubt that reverse engineering and copying have played a very large role in China's technological feats, particularly in the military sector, as anyone who glances through the Cox Committee Report, or reads Richard Fisher or the Russian military press can see. According to the Cox Committee Report, China's agencies maintain close surveillance on foreign technologies imported into the PRC through joint ventures and practice a coordinated strategy to strip-mine technology assets from any and every source they can access. In an example of diverting civilian imports from their end use to military purposes, the Cox Committee reported that machine tools meant for the co-production of MD-82 and MD-90 civil commercial aircraft by McDonnell Douglas and China National Aero-Technology Import and Export Corporation (CATIC) in China were 'diverted to Nanchang Aircraft Company, which was "known to manufacture military

16. *The Competitive Advantage of Nations* (New York: Free Press, 1990).

aircraft and cruise missile components, as well as commercial products" in violation of "key conditions in the licenses".' McDonnell Douglas also appears to have provided large amounts of technical data and training to Chinese workers in the process.

In fact, China has officially made known, the priority it places to reverse engineer technology. A full section of the 'Guidelines for the Medium- and Long-Term National Science and Technology [S&T] Development Programme (2006-2020)' is devoted to exhorting the country to 'enhance the absorption, assimilation, and re-innovation of imported technologies'. Further, Chinese leaders and leading officials regularly refer to this priority in their speeches.

Late industrialising countries usually have the option of following the path of 'absorption', as Cheung observes, and can do so with success if they have a purposeful strategic direction, which we in India sadly lack. According to him '"Absorption can come in a number of forms" and "imitation has been instrumental in the successful development of newly industrializing economies in Asia".'

Re-engineering of Government

China visibly switched priorities, redirecting its efforts to build economic prosperity by implementing an entire series of reforms meant to free its potential. Prof Cheung describes the strenuous efforts for defence conversion. China has also experimented with re-engineering government, state structures and the state led economy in order to create a more synergised and focussed instrument capable of directing and facilitating innovation and science and technological development. An excellent description of this programme is contained in Prof Cheung's book *Fortifying China* (2009). Without the systematic reforms which it has implemented China could not have sustained technological innovation after the initial phase of copying was over, and it could not have achieved the successes described in the section above.

Lessons for India

China has climbed up the technology ladder in the first place, because it has a national vision for achieving technological power, implementing a single-minded policy to study, monitor, copy and assimilate foreign technologies, and implementing reforms throughout its economy, educational, industrial and state organisation structures in order to absorb these and support independent technological innovation and discovery. Thus after the copying phase, China has developed its own abilities and advanced beyond being a system integrator to a technology producer. As we have seen, China has additionally used the civilian route as a very helpful conduit for the importation of dual-use technologies. In automotive, telecommunications, civil aircraft, railways, China has used variants of a simple strategy with variable levels of success:

A: Import technology and reverse engineer]
P: Roll out own product] = APE
E: Export]

End result: Increase comprehensive national power including national welfare through increased employment, productivity, more value added production and high-tech supply networks and therefore better remuneration for labour and higher living standards.

China is an authoritarian country which has certain means at its disposal which are not available to countries like India. The extraordinary re-engineering of government structures and the capability to make the frequent reorganisations and reforms actually work, also require a greater degree of authoritarian control which is lacking in India. But there are many areas in which we can learn lessons from China, since its success is also dependent on commercialising the military production process.

China is in the process of establishing a viable National Innovation System (NIS). They have the capability to produce internationally competitive products including defence equipment. They are a formidable force because they are firmly positioned on the high-tech manufacturing highway.

It should be evident that India also needs to acquire high-tech capabilities if it wants to play a role commensurate with its size and potential on the international stage and sustain productive strategic alliances with its partners. India has made advances in some sectors like remote sensing, IT, automotive components, pharmaceuticals and shipbuilding, and even to some extent in the defence industry sector with a light combat aircraft and the main battle tank recently being accepted by the armed forces for induction, *albeit* the reports state that these are still dependent on imported content. And it cannot be any other way until India develops its own manufacturing and innovative capabilities. A sophisticated technological product requires sophisticated and intricate supply chains composed of myriad high-precision, high-quality inputs. This is typical of advanced economies and this combination of factors is what gives them their competitive advantage over technological backwards, as brilliantly explained two decades ago by Michael Porter in his *Competitive Advantage of Nations* (1990). Indian excellence in a few sectors is not an economy-wide phenomenon due to the lack of a national innovation system and low R&D to GDP ratio (0.9% as estimated by Adams *et al.*, 2009).

There is a pressing need for urgent action on this front, as restrictions on tech transfer are being removed by the US and other friendly countries. The Indo-US joint statement promises the end of technology denial regimes and removal of Indian companies from the entities list. India can hopefully soon access advanced technologies and moreover the implicit proscribing of CMI in India should gradually disappear. This could be a revolutionary development but only if we do not miss the opportunity to develop our own technological capabilities to be able to absorb these fresh infusions. Because as restrictions on exports ease, we will be able to access machine tools and other advanced equipment which were earlier not allowed to be exported to India. Our import dependence may increase even more. This is a real danger. If this were China, these inputs would be diverted to the military sector or used on common assembly lines for both military and civil production and the technology absorbed. It is important for Indian enterprises to start the process of indigeneous innovation, assimilation and reverse engineering otherwise it will only increase our dependency on foreign products and technology.

Given the worldwide preoccupation with retaining or attaining technological supremacy, it is strange that no realisation on the urgency of having a national technology policy seems to be evident in India, even though a growing technological gap, especially with China, bodes ill for India.

It is imperative that India finds a strategy for fast and massive technological upgradation so it can develop a high-tech manufacturing sector and meet the challenges and security dilemmas of the 21st century. This should be based on rapid expansion of manufacturing, through defence offsets, FDI and any other means available, accompanied by an indigeneous drive to produce cutting edge technologies, since no one will part with high-end technologies.

Recommendations

Indigeneous Efforts

Rely primarily on indigeneous efforts to create a sound R&D base and system for technological innovation. China's experience in creating a diversified manufacturing base and an aerospace sector that is part of international supply networks holds many lessons for India, but the key takeaway is that a country has to first and foremost rely on indigeneous efforts to ensure long-term success. India should thus declare creation of a viable innovation system based on solid R&D foundations and indigeneous high-tech manufacturing a national priority. India needs a National Vision for an Integrated Science & Technology Advancement Strategy (VISTAS) prioritising the indigeneous development of technology directed by India's leadership at the highest levels, and a corresponding government structure that can implement the goals.

India should re-engineer government structures to ensure priority for the indigeneous development of technology in major imports, purchase, procurement orders, etc. India should increase the target for R&D expenditure to 2 per cent of GDP by 2015 and 3 per cent by 2025.

Expand Manufacturing

India's manufacturing sector has to be expanded because technological innovation can thrive only on a diversified manufacturing base. China's example is very instructive as it first implemented massive economic reforms, then experimented with defence conversion and finally adopted the CMI model in order to leverage the potential of both its advanced economic manufacturing sector for its defence sector and vice versa. For India too the effort has therefore to start with upgrading the civilian economy and expanding its manufacturing sector.

Manufacturing needs governance reforms, infrastructure and labour reforms and reduction of the absurd legacies of the 'Inspection Raj'. Foreign partnership is of course desirable, but the focus should be on starting with and focussing on domestic reforms and indigenisation in a non-autarkic framework, however challenging these may be.

Civil Military Integration

Thereafter, India needs to move away from compartmentalised paradigms, to one which encompasses civil and military integration, utilising the 'spin-on' effects of an upgraded civilian economy for the defence production sector and vice versa. Most of the major advanced countries have created dual-use economic infrastructure in their countries, recognising the importance of synergies between the two sectors. This is not surprising as even a simple product requires thousands of parts in the form of advanced circuitry, components, composite materials etc. India needs to adopt a similar approach and create a sophisticated dual-use manufacturing sector.

Indian Industry should spend at least 5 per cent of Revenues on R&D

In all advanced economies, industry pays more than 60 per cent of national R&D costs. Small and medium enterprises (SMEs) should also be empowered to conduct R&D and find a market for their products. Government must devise procedures to create a market for SME products.

Transparency

All facilitating ministries should have the names and contact details of officials directly responsible for clearances and facilitation of indigeneous industry and R&D. They should be given incentives for achieving R&D indigenisation targets.

Reform Defence Offsets Regime

Far reaching defence sector reforms, particularly in the offsets regime, which should be extended to the entire economy, have to be implemented. One way to achieve this is to reform the defence offsets regime.

Increase Offsets to 100 per cent

Under offsets, foreign companies have to invest up to 30 per cent in production of defence-related equipment in India. This should be increased to 100 per cent, as this will encourage a massive shift of manufacturing to India. This is not uncommon, with the Jane's Industrial Quarterly[17]

17. "The Changing Role of Offset in the Global Defence Market", *Jane's Industry Quarterly*, 3 November 2009.

citing Brazil, Argentina and the UK (which calls for 100 per cent industrial participation) as countries that make a stipulation of 100 per cent on offsets/industrial participation.

Reserve 30-50 per cent for the Defence Production Sector

The commitment to the defence production sector must not be diluted under an expanded offsets regime.

Allow Indirect Offsets for the Rest 50-70 per cent

The defence offsets policy could provide a very valuable route for reform. Jane's has analysed the offsets regimes globally and concluded that some East and Central European countries have used indirect offsets 'to foster wider economic development of emerging economies; to increase participation in global markets through exports; and to accelerate the development of local skills and technological capabilities.'[18]

The whole philosophy of restricting offsets to only the defence sector perpetuates the compartmentalised paradigm which is not beneficial to the overall upgradation of the economy.

Make Offsets Mandatory for Every Major Purchase

100 per cent offsets should also be mandatory for all massive equipment purchases across all possible sectors.

Ensure Transparency in Measuring Offsets

Transparent and measurable methodologies such as those adopted by other countries must be adopted in India to encourage transfer of technology.

Increase FDI Cap to 51 per cent

The cap on foreign investment which has been set at 26 per cent should be increased at least to 51 per cent so that manufacturing facilities are set up in India, as the FDI cap ensures that no company really bring high-end technology, unless it has control. It is better that the system is manufactured in India, thus generating employment and other spin-offs, as

---

18. Ibid.

against importing the entire unit from abroad. At the same time, we should mandate technology transfer and phased indigenisation as a condition.

Set up Vocational Education Programmes under Offsets

Other suggestions that can be explored is for foreign companies to set up a vocational education (VE) training system under offsets by which we can educate millions and millions of young unemployed engineering graduates and others in vocational training. We can also consider copying the German system of universities of applied sciences which also equip people for manufacturing jobs. Basically the aim should be to create a growing manufacturing sector which has a larger share of the Indian economy. The Chinese are considering opening up VE to FDI.

Integrate Scientific and Educational Infrastructure

Much needed reforms in the scientific infrastructure of the country, as well as in the education sector, both higher education and vocational have to be carried out urgently. An important complement to China's high-tech strategy (and defence structural reforms) was simultaneous initiatives in higher education through the 211 and 985 programmers.

R&D Investment has to be Increased and Systems Reformed

India should consider freeing its defence research laboratories to find their own income streams, incentivise the private sector to invest in innovation, restructure government agencies dealing with innovation by investing a technology council with overarching powers over civil and military economic processes. For example, promotion criteria should be skewed towards scientists who are able to bring their technologies to the market, rather than simply publish irrelevant research papers. This is not to detract from outstanding basic research, but just to provide a little market-driven focus and criteria into our moribund, non-meritocratic systems.

One innovation that other countries have undertaken is to empower their universities to do marketable research. These reforms have started in a small way at India's universities particularly our IITs. This process should be encouraged and strengthened so that people are rewarded for innovation.

Change Culture: Promote Innovation

There is also need for a culture which genuinely promotes youthful exuberance, a questioning and creative mindset, innovation, people who are pushing at the envelope. More often than not, India's geriatric culture suppresses good ideas, talent and dynamic people. Mediocrity therefore rules and drives India's best abroad.

That's another area where China's example is worth studying since it reformed cumbersome internal structures and systems and created an environment for systemic innovation. India should focus on the spin on aspects more than the spin-off, since the intuitive understanding that Deng had was that military technology requirements could to a great deal be satisfied from the civilian economy.

Caveats

Some sectors, such as civil nuclear energy and space will continue to work behind firewalls, as mandated in the Indo-US nuclear deal, and many other entities may need to preserve their 'civil' classification, but no externally mandated fiat should prevent Indians from developing their own capabilities, or from benefitting from global commerce in technology products.

These recommendations are not aimed as an elitist exercise to create a high-tech economy for the exclusive enjoyment of the upper classes—excluding our suffering and immiserated masses, whose lives provide grim inspiration for tragi-comedies like *Peepli Live*. They are aimed at creating a sound foundation for higher employment with rapid growth and technological progress, all of which also constitute the foundations of our national security.

The outlines of a possible growth strategy which improves national welfare even as it strengthens national security has been suggested. The crucial issue of agricultural sector reforms has not been dealt with here—which was one of the starting points for China's own economic reforms and which are crucially needed in India to improve national welfare—but this is similarly an area which should command the priority attention of our policymakers. Export economists will need to apply themselves to the issues thrown up and the optimal strategies for development, but we can help initiate this process by thinking about and acting on the examples set by China and others). In any case, the centrality of the fact that we are already years behind China needs to occupy centre stage in our national debate, given that China has lately shown signs of pushing the envelope when it comes to our 'core concerns'.

References

Adams, Jonathan, Christopher King and Vinay Singh (2009)."The New Geography of Science: Research and Collaboration in India", *Thomson Reuters Global Research Report*. October.

Cliff, Roger, J. Chad, R. Ohlandt and David Yang (2011). *Ready for Take-off: China's Advancing Aerospace Industry*. Monograph sponsored by the U.S.-China Economic and Security Review Commission, Rand National Security Research Division. *http://www.rand.org/content/dam/rand/pubs/monographs/2011/RAND_MG1100.pdf*

Cheung, Tai Ming (2009). *Fortifying China*. Cornell University Press.

China Daily (2002). "China to become Aircraft Parts Manufacture Center", *China Daily* (11.07.2002).

Dingding, Xin (2010). "High-Speed Rail Links to be Doubled by 2012", *China Daily*, Updated: 2010-07-29. *http://usa.chinadaily.com.cn/2010-07/29/content_11068529.htm*

GoI (2011). *Strategy for Doubling Exports in Next Three Years (2011-12 to 2013-14)*. New Delhi: Ministry of Commerce & Industry, Department of Commerce. *http://commerce.nic.in/whatsnew/StrategyPaper.pdf*

Goldstein, Andrea (2005). *The Political Economy of Industrial Policy in China: The Case of Aircraft Manufacturing*. OECD Development Centre, July; also as *William Davidson Institute Working Papers Series* 779, William Davidson Institute at the University of Michigan, Stephen M. Ross Business School.

Grevatt, Jon (2001). "China Drafts FDI Plan for Defence Sector", *Jane's Asia-Pacific Industry Reporter*, 8 April.

Hsiao, Russell (2011). "Twelfth-Five Year Plan Accelerates Civil-Military Integration in China's Defense Industry", *China Brief* 11(1), January 14.

Moran, Theodore H. (2011). "Foreign Manufacturing Multinationals and the Transformation of the Chinese Economy: New Measurements, New Perspectives", *Working Paper Series*, WP 11, April 11.

Office of the Secretary of Defence (2009). *Annual Report to Congress: Military Power of the People's Republic of China*.

Page, Jeremy (2011). "China Eyes U.S. Defense Contracts", *The Wall Street Journal*, February 4.

Pasztor, Andy and Norihiko Shirouzu (2009). "Chinese Jet Gets Boost From Obama", *The Wall Street Journal*, November 20.

People's Daily (2010). "Boeing Invests 7.5 million USD in Tsinghua Research Center", *People's Daily*, October 21.

Planning Commission (2011). "State of Economy & Prospects", *Economic Survey 2010-11*. Chapter 1. Government of India.

Purushottam, Smita (2010a). "China goes Hi-tech, IPR Infringements and all", *Business Standard*, October 03, 2010. *http://www.business-standard.com/india/news/smita-purushottam-china-goes-hi-tech-ipr-infringementsall/409971/*

Purushottam, Smita (2010b). "A Growing Technological Gap with China?", *Strategic Analysis* 34(4): 496–503, July.

Qingfen, Ding (2011). "China 'Opening Wider' for Foreign Investment", *China Daily*, 8 April.

4 China's Environmental Problems

An Indian Viewpoint

P.S. Ramakrishnan

Introduction

China and India are the two most rapidly growing economic powers in the Asian region. China had an early start towards industrialisation, as part of its post-cultural revolution, while India pitched in only a little over a decade ago. From an environmental perspective, both India and China have had a long history of exploitation of their natural resources largely arising from pressures external to the region; in more recent times this has been fuelled from within to support the ongoing industrialisation process. This has had its adverse impact on the otherwise richly endowed natural resource base of China as well as India, also leading to rapidly rising industrial pollution. The environmental problems that China faces today are similar to what is happening in the Indian context. However, the solutions to the problems that the two countries face will possibly have to be qualitatively somewhat different, largely arising from the two distinct political models that differentiate these two emerging economies. This is the comparative context in which environmental issues in China and the solutions to their problems, have to be viewed.

Growing Urban Sprawl, Industrialisation and Linked Pollution

Overwhelming urbanisation of the landscape is a leading element in the emerging (regional) scenario. China has outstripped India in this respect. During the last few decades, conversion of arable land into urban sprawls has become a matter of concern; the rate at which this has occurred in the Pearl River Delta region, which once used to be a major grain basket of China, is indeed a glaring example of the kind of problems that face this region. According to China's governmental estimates, some 200,000 hectares of arable land in China is estimated to be disappearing each year due to urbanisation and industrialisation. It is projected that by 2030, China could have 828 million city dwellers, if the present rate of urbanisation continues. A major population problem arising from all this is a large floating population in the Pearl River Delta, and a similar project in the Jitai Basin, the grain basket of China.[1] The situation in India is not very different, with urban sprawls and linked pollution problems increasing rapidly in expanding metropolis like Mumbai, Delhi, Kolkata and Chennai.

Arising from uncontrolled urbanisation is also the problem of developing huge urban slums. Increasing problems linked with urban waste disposal and pollution levels in the air water and on land are all that contribute to a generally poorer quality of life for the vast majority of the population in the two emerging economies. This big divide between the rich and the poor also contribute towards rapidly emerging human security issues in these urban sprawls. However, unlike in the Chinese context, in India vibrant environmental activism has taken root through a well-developed NGO network. India has a pronounced bottom-up approach for problem-solving which augurs well for effectively addressing sustainability concerns, involving all stakeholders.

Industrialisation and urbanisation have resulted in a profound deterioration of the quality of air both in India and China, the main sources being vehicular emissions and untreated dirty coal-based industrial smoke, and the absence of adequate pollution control mechanisms. With about 251 million metric tons of carbon equivalent emitted in 2001, India is fifth in the world in carbon emissions, behind the United States, China, Russia and Japan. However, India's per capita carbon emissions is relatively low—at 0.25 metric tonnes of carbon per person in 2001.[2] India's per capita carbon emissions were less than one-quarter of the world average and 22 times less than the United States. In other words, India is fifth in the world in carbon emissions, behind the USA, China, Russia and Japan. According to one informed estimate,[3] China's rapid industrialisation will lead to

1. Wolman *et al.* (2001).
2. *http://eia.doe.gov/emeu/cabs/indiaenv.html*
3. http://en.wikipedia.org/Environment_of_China

increased carbon dioxide emission into the atmosphere exceeding that of the USA by 2010; China will then account for 39 per cent of the increase in carbon dioxide, as its emissions more than double in the period to 2030. This is largely because it is dependent on 'dirty' coal-fired power stations for its electrical power, rather than relatively clean gas-fuelled plants. The International Energy Agency (IEA), which advises industrialised countries, has predicted that global carbon dioxide emissions would increase by 55 per cent between now and 2030, unless tackled effectively, from now on.

From a global perspective, the IEA in one of its latest reports has estimated that China would become the world's top emitter of greenhouse gases by 2030.[4] In this context, IEA has recommended a rapid expansion in the use of renewable energy sources, including biofuels for vehicles. It says nuclear power could also make a major contribution to cutting fuel imports and curbing CO_2 emissions, but only if governments facilitate a push for private investment in this area. It is heartening to see the rapidly emerging Indo-US collaboration in the area of atomic energy use for peaceful purposes. The IEA predicts that even if the suggested steps are taken, CO_2 emissions will continue to rise, but will be 16 per cent less than with business as usual approach. If effective policy action from governments is not forthcoming, IEA sums up, energy demand and CO_2 emissions could both increase by more than 50 per cent, threatening severe and irreversible environmental damage, with severe ecological and economic consequences. Strangely enough, however, China now being the second largest emitter, has implicitly taken the position that by controlling its population based on one-child per family norm, it is actually contributing to global environmental health,[5] a position that is controversial and unfortunate.

In the area of environmental activism, though the non-governmental sector is still weak in China unlike in India, there seems to be a growing movement in China towards organised collective action through the available legitimate channels. In other words, Chinese workers are trying to exert mass pressure within the existing hierarchical power structure, rather than challenging it from outside, which implies that China is not likely to create an independent civil society and move towards democratic

4. "World Faces 'Dirty, Insecure' Energy Future", *www.newscientist.com*
5. *http:/en.wikipedia. org/wiki/kyoto_protocol*

governance in the near future.[6] No doubt, China's leaders are concerned with environmental protection, but they have been unable or unwilling to take the necessary political and economic steps to reverse the overall negative trends China is confronted with, on environmental degradation and pollution on the ground.[7] This is the context in which the efforts of the Chinese government to develop Environmental Protection Industry (EPI), and the recommendations of the draft report of the China Council for International Cooperation on Environment and Development (CCICED) Task Force (2003) on financial mechanisms to promote environmental protection, become debatable though these involve interesting initiatives.

Rapidly Degrading Natural Resource Base

With uncontrolled population pressure and industrialisation, one of the major casualties in both India and China has been the natural resource base—biodiversity and the closely linked water resource base. There is an increasing evidence to indicate that biodiversity as an important natural resource is the key to enable humans to cope with rapidly emerging environmental uncertainties. This applies particularly to the marginalised sections of the society. This trend is getting aggravated by 'global change' (climate change and global warming, land use and cover changes, biodiversity depletion and biological invasion by alien exotic species) as an ecological phenomenon[8] and 'globalisation' of economies.[9] In this context, sustainable management of water resources, and making it available to local communities, urban, rural and traditional, could act as a trigger for conserving and indeed enhancing biodiversity in all its scalar dimenions—sub-species (varieties), species, ecosystems and landscapes). This is the context in what follows has to be viewed.

Land Use/Land Cover Changes

Working with shifting agricultural (*jhum*) farmers in northeastern hill areas of India, this author had concluded that this traditional land use

6. Asia Program (2004).
7. Economy (2004).
8. Bondeau *et al.* (1997).
9. Dragun and Tisdell (1999).

system is sustainable if left to itself, and to dub it as 'primitive' would be not appropriate, further the indication is that *jhum* farmers are not the key drivers of deforestation.[10] This is also applicable to Yunnan province of China situated directly opposite on the other side of the border of NE India. The truth is that it is not these small farmers, but the timber extractors operating on a larger scale and coming from outside the region which are the real perpetrators for deforestation and land degradation.

That external pressures from outside the region for industrial use of the timber are to a large extent responsible for large-scale deforestation. That poverty and local population pressures are not the key drivers of land use/cover has been confirmed in the funding of the tri-Academy collaborative project involving India, China and USA, with two regional case studies from each of the three countries.[11] What this study showed was in an increasingly globalised world, places are linked more strongly over greater distances. Market pressures, both national and international are the key drivers that determine land use/cover changes, and population and poverty at best could only be seen as proximal drivers of lesser magnitude impacting upon an already damaged landscape. It is therefore surprising that a detailed literature review done on this topic under the international 'global change' programme has perpetuated the myth of poverty and local population pressures as the main factors making for deforestation and land degradation.

Changing 'Waterscape'

Water is a key issue not only for sustainability of land use practices with implications for food security, but also for sustainable landscape management with concerns for biodiversity. With the monsoon climate determining skewed water availability during the year, sustainable management of water is a key issue for the region. Intensively managed energy-intensive agriculture has been a major factor for sub-surface aquifer water depletion in the region, apart from exploitation of water for meeting with ever-increasing industrial demands. This situation is further complicated by manipulation of larger perennial water bodies for hydro-electric power generation, leading to unsustainable scenarios (Box 4.1).

10. Ramakrishnan (1992a) and Ramakrishnan *et al.* (2006).

11. Wolman *et al.* (2001).

Box 4.1

Depleting Water Resources

- In China, water tables are falling almost everywhere, where the land is flat, ...particularly in the northern half of the country which is literally drying out. This is a region that accounts for nearly 40 per cent of China's grain harvest; the water table is falling by roughly 1.5 m per year.
- The Yellow River, the cradle of Chinese civilisation, going intermittently dry, ran completely dry for the first time in China's 3,000-year history in 1972, failing to reach the sea for some 15 days. In 1997, however, it failed to reach the sea for seven months out of the year.
- With hundreds of major projects planned in upstream provinces to withdraw water for industrial and urban use, for power projects, and for irrigation, the Yellow River could one day become an inland river, never reaching the sea.
- The Indian scenario is no better, even though 'green revolution' agriculture is confined to a small segment of the Indian plains. The extraction of water from aquifers is projected to exceed recharge by a factor of 2 or more, with the freshwater aquifers being pulled down by 1-3 metres per year.
- Farmers in the Indian state of Gujarat, for example, are drilling their irrigation wells some 1.5 m deeper each year in a futile pursuit of rapidly falling water tables, unless sufficient recovery period is offered for restoring the water table.
- In India, state governments give cheap or free electricity to farmers, who use it to pump water out of underground aquifers faster than natural recharge through rains, recharging them. Though the subsidies are often defended in the name of the poor farmer or the urban food buyer, most of the money ends up in the pockets of richer farmers, who can afford electric pumps.

Source: Brown *et al.* (1999).

Meanwhile, during the last few decades, damming rivers has been seen as a quick-fix solution to compensate for the rapidly depleting groundwater resources, not only for agricultural intensification but also to meet with the increasing energy needs arising from industrialisation. Increased water availability on a large scale is also seen as a way to alter the cropping patterns in tune with changing market demands even if altered cropping regimes entails high water demand. The problems that have arisen from intensive rice-wheat rotational cropping systems done in the name of the 'green revolution' that has put stress on limited water resources available in the Punjab, Haryana and Western Uttar Pradesh is a case in point. Industrialisation of agriculture as a response to increasing market pressures in the Chinese context too, for e.g., in the Jitai Basin and the Pearl River Delta regions has brought in its wake rapid degradation of the landscape too.[12] At the other end of the spectrum, both countries have large tracts of arid land. In both countries, sustainability of even traditional dryland agriculture is becoming more and more a critical issue, of rapidly breaking-down traditional dryland farming practices, and they are being replaced with energy intensive farming practices. With all these drastic and unsustainable land use changes happening in the region, damming rivers has been seen as a way out meeting for essential irrigation requirements thus compensating for the rapidly depleting groundwater resources. In short, increasing population pressure and market demands in the region have raised a whole range of issues linked with reviving agriculture based on agroforestry principles.

It is pertinent at this stage to have a brief statement on the damming of rivers that cut across national boundaries; possibilities of damming of the river Brahmaputra at its origin on the Chinese side of the border is an issue of concern in recent times. With a large population living across the border in northeastern India and Bangladesh, food security is under threat. At another level, excess availability of water in the otherwise arid zone like Tibetan plateau could sooner or later, raise issues connected with energy-intensive and unsustainable land use, diversification and intensification, a situation which is being faced in the alluvial plains of Punjab and Haryana, emerging from excessive use of water and inorganic fertilisers in the context of 'green revolution' agriculture. On the social side, this could lead to human suffering, with conflicts across national boundaries.

It is in this context that the ongoing discussion in India, at governmental and non-governmental levels, on the subject of damming and interlinking of rivers, so as to enable water availability over larger regions of the country for intensified agriculture and other uses, even in rainfall deficient regions, has to be seen. Given an unevenly distributed monsoon rainfall situation, across space and time, such a project may seem to be justifiable; but in fact, a closer scrutiny of its implications raises serious

12. Wolman *et al.* (2001).

issues linked with sustainable soil fertility management, as demonstrated in the 'green revolution' agricultural areas of Haryana and Punjab regions in northwestern India.[13] Such large-scale manipulations of river water may also have implications on coastal mangrove ecosystems and marine coastal biodiversity too. To sum up this, one should question the wisdom of large-scale manipulations of river systems that are currently happening in the India-China context; the indication is that such alterations will indeed contribute towards exacerbating environmental uncertainties arising from global change issues.

Coping with Global Environmental Change: Where do we Stand?

Industrial Pollution Control

In the area of industrial pollution control, the two countries have a long way to go, though there has been an increasing interest in both countries on clean technologies. India's high concentration of pollution is not due to the absence of a sound environmental legal regime, but due to enforcement-related issues at the local level. With an environmentally proactive Supreme Court, and a long established non-governmental environmental watchdog well in place, controlling environmental pollution in the Indian context does offer some hope for the future. On the contrary, with a well-entrenched 'top-down' approach in the decision-making process and with emphasis being on rapid industrialisation at any cost, to what extent the action plan contained in the Chinese governmental document[14] will get implemented is debatable, at this juncture.

Sustainable Natural Resource Management: An Environmental Buffer

Arising from the increasing realisation now that sustainable management of natural resource management with emphasis on conserving and sustainably managing biodiversity is a key buffering mechanism available with us to cope up with pollution-related issues, sustainable management of biodiversity at the landscape level is being seen as an

13. Ramakrishnan (2001) and Ramakrishnan *et al.* (2005).

14. Information Office of the State Council of the People's Republic of China (2006).

effective buffer against pollution-related impacts. In other words, mitigation efforts in the two countries have to be promoted through appropriately designed carbon-sequestration measures that are community participatory, an effort that is now getting increasing international attention. This effort is helped by increasing realisation that 'knowledge systems'—'traditional ecological knowledge' (TEK) has also to be taken on board along with the textbook based 'formal knowledge' that we have used so far.[15] Such a linkage between knowledge systems to evolve sustainable management technologies is being seen more and more as the key to relate to a value system that local communities understand and appreciate and therefore are able to participate in an environmental conservation-linked sustainable developmental process. Such an approach will not only address a whole range of direct benefits that communities could derive through sustainable management of timber and non-timber forest products (NTFPs), but also throw the light on the range of indirect benefits that could accrue through sustainable water and soil fertility management and linked nutrient cycling processes within the ecosystem/landscape.

Sustainable Water Management

In order to ensure water availability which is becoming a critical issue in the contemporary context increasing demand for a variety of reasons, the tendency in the region is to ensure availability of this declining resource through large-scale manipulation of river systems. Whilst this is a 'quick-fix' solution, the two countries do have a rich tradition of small-scale community-based water management. In the Indian context, for one has to note the move towards, revival of traditional water harvesting technologies where available,[16] and creating small-scale cheap water harvesting systems where such a tradition no more exists,[17] which are rapidly emerging as environmental-friendly possibilities; NGOs, are the key players in such de-centralised efforts. What is emerging in the Indian context is an approach which requires an appropriate balance between the 'big' operating on a regional scale and the 'small' at the local level. When one realises that community-centred small-scale efforts could keep

15. Ramakrishnan (1993; 2001) and Ramakrishnan *et al.* (2005).
16. Agarwal and Narain (1997).
17. Kothyari *et al.* (1991).

in check large-scale manipulations of river systems, such an approach offers immense possibilities for sustainable water resource management. This also opens up possibilities for cooperation between India and China, with implications for sustainable water security for the region as a whole. Such an integrated approach towards water resource management that will promote conservation of both aboveground and belowground biodiversity, which will be a powerful tool to control pollution-related problems too. It is against this background that the following suggestions for action in the area of sustainable natural resource management for pollution abatement in the landscape (natural forests and human-managed agricultural systems) through sustainable carbon sequestration becomes important.

Sustainable Land Use Systems Management

With only about a forest cover of around 20 per cent, it is becoming obvious that both countries have to go a long way towards building a secure forest cover to combat problems emerging from the still ongoing deforestation, (though now on progressively driven by scale), in the name of rapid industrialisation. Further, much of the afforestation programmes are largely focussed around plantation forestry taken up by traditional foresters; hence these efforts are delinked from community concerns in forestry, and therefore have only served the limited purpose of increasing tree cover. Through such a conservative approach, China claims to have added 6.67 million ha of afforested area per year.[18] India, on the other hand, claims to have created a more modest average of about 8-9 million ha of forest plantations on over a five-year period, during the Seventh and Eighth Five Year Plan. Being largely delinked from forest dwellers, forestry programmes that has followed a centralised 'top-down' approach have often led to alienation of forest dwellers.

With increasing awareness about the need to integrate the socio-ecological and the cultural dimension for sustainability of forestry practices, the realisation towards community-centred TEK has started gaining foresters' attention over the last few decades.[19] The rich TEK base linked with an equally rich eco-cultural diversity forms the basis for using socially

18. Information Office of the State Council of the People's Republic of China (2006); GoI (1999).

19. Ramakrishnan (1992b).

valued and ecologically significant keystone species is being seen as a powerful tool[20] to ensure community participation; this forms an important foundation for sustainable forestry global initiative of the International Union of Forest Research Organization (IUFRO) in which the South Asian region has a key role to play.[21] This is the context in which some of the emerging initiatives in the Indian context has to be seen (Box 4.2).

Replicability of such isolated experiences on a larger scale requires appropriate institutional arrangements for project implementation based on community values. From the point of view of forest dwellers, revival of traditional institutional arrangements can ensure effective community participation, based on a value system that the communities understand and appreciate, thus provides an inducement to participate in such land use management initiatives. One of the first successful attempts to redevelop the shifting agriculture affected landscape, is the project taken up in Nagaland in northeast India, addressing sustainable forestry-linked food security for the people living there. Now known as the Nagaland Environment Protection and Economic Development (NEPED) project, involving 1,200 villages of Nagaland, this community participatory initiative was based on agroforestry principles, on community values as expressed through the TEK which they had in an abundant measure; socially valued tree species with linked ecological keystone value, was the basis for such a redeveloped agroforestry system initiative. This found immediate acceptance from the local farmers in the region.[22]

The very principles that socially valued species have: an ecological keystone value in terms of improving soil fertility through organic residue recycling, which formed the basis for the NEPED project of Nagaland, as well as for the organic residue management strategies followed for the tea plantation industry in the Western Ghat mountain regions in southern India. This approach helps bring about a standardisation of a sustainable soil fertility management technology. Such an approach has drastically reduced the dependence of the farmer on excessive use of inorganic fertilisers. In other words, the net result was sustainable soil fertility management with

20. Ramakrishnan (1996); Ramakrishnan *et al.* (1998).

21. Parrotta *et al.* (2008).

22. Ramakrishnan (2001).

Box 4.2

A Few Examples of Isolated Initiatives in the Indian Context

- What happened in the 1980s as the National Tree Growers' Cooperative Federation, a bottom-up initiative in the Indian context, over a period of time has been able to get a deeper understanding of location-specific land use-based social realities, and has been able to get community participation in rural forestry-based restoration of degraded lands. Though recent reports suggest that the forest cover in India and China is on the increase, sustainable rural forestry needs to be get much more and more focussed around local values through TEK available with communities.
- In the area of watershed management, there also exist isolated examples of community participatory approaches. One of the earliest attempts in India to have an integrated land use development linked with water management, with community participation, was the one attempted in the Himalayan foothills of the Siwaliks, near Chandigarh in north-west India. Using an Institution, the Hill Resource Management Society (HRMS) as the driver, water conservation measures were initiated through earthen check dams, to cope up with erratic rainfall, and the consequent severe shortage of water for agriculture. The Sukhomajri model redeveloping the existing agriculture, animal husbandry, horticulture and fisheries, linked it with rural forestry initiative, thus, created an ecological buffer. HRMS, with membership provided for each household, was used as the instrument for conflict resolution.
- Reviving the traditional 'Johads', dug-out tanks with earthen embankments, to store the limited rain water of the monsoon season in the semi-arid, drought-prone Alwar District of Rajasthan in northwest India, with a highly committed NGO, Tarun Bharat Sangh, the Alwar region now boasts of over 3,000 such tanks spread over 650 villages. Increased underground seepage, and the consequent rise in water table, arising out of this massive effort has helped in regenerating half a dozen seasonal rivulets and establishing perennial systems. Besides this, there are also economic benefits for local communities through improved land quality, and the consequent changes brought about in cropping and other land use systems, animal husbandry, and many other indirect benefits brought in by the community managed forests that have been regenerated with water management acting as the key element.

Source: Ramakrishnan (2001).

improved productivity, both in a qualitative and quantitative sense, in this case of tea leaves. The patented technology for sustainable soil fertility management has gone to China.[23]

In the two examples on Nagaland and the Western Ghat situations noted above, formal knowledge-based technologies for agriculture had to be moderated with TEK-linked inputs, to address sustainability concerns. This renewed interest in the development of sustainable agroforestry system models has led to a renewed interest in integrated agroforestry-based farming system models, both in India[24] and China,[25] where the objective has been to curtail, to the extent possible, external energy subsidies for agriculture through increased tree cover in the landscape.

General Considerations

The Asian–Australian monsoon is an important component of the Earth's climate system that influences the societal and economic activity of roughly half the world's population. Recent studies suggest that changing monsoon patterns in the past has contributed to human migrations in the tropical rain belt, which for example was one of the factors leading to the decline of the Tang dynasty in China.[26] However, those changes that occurred in the past are on a geological time-scale. What we are witnessing today on a global scale are increasing environmental uncertainties and the consequences of ecological 'global change' and economic globalisation. With new emerging industrialised economies like the most populous India and China coming on the scene, along with the developed world, the environmental uncertainties will only get further magnified, unless these emerging countries are supported by the developed world and the already industrialised world make their own moves towards global environmental protection. Having said that, these two developing countries themselves too have to strengthen the process of internal dialogue in the area of environmental protection linked with sustainable development. This is where the role of the NGO sector, in the area of awareness generation

23. Senapati *et al.* (2002).
24. Chadha and Swaminathan (2006).
25. Wenhua (2001).
26. Yancheva *et al.* (2007).

amongst all stakeholders, acting as checks and balances in the area of governmental decision-making processes at all levels is relevant.

NGO Movement in the Two Countries

In the Chinese context, during the 'cultural revolution', human conquest of 'nature' was a popular theme, though this situation has somewhat changed now. In recent times, there is an increasing awareness in China about the progressive degradation of its environment. China today is experiencing dynamic environmentalism but with no environmental movement; simply stated, right across the Chinese society there is an increasing concern for the environment, but with little environmental activism. In other words, Chinese environmentalism fails to conform to the definition of a social movement, though environmental conflicts do arise. From a situation where the Chinese media had a superficial covering of governmental reports and events like tree planting activities, in recent times, it is not uncommon to find articles critical of the government. However, the environmental media still remains controlled. Though the educated youth do recognise the gravity of China's environmental dilemma and through this has led to a few instances of student participation in environmental campaigns, these still remain isolated exceptions. The Chinese state has taken a few steps, though not enough, in recent years to address environmental issues, with some success however this remain inadequate. In recent times, web-based environmental activism through the most influential NGO 'Friends of Nature', is quietly underway.[27] Subsequently launched 'green-web' and 'Han Hai Sha' are some of the other initiatives that have had isolated local impacts. These efforts give some hope for the future in harmonising the 'top-down' decision-making process of the Chinese political leadership, with the much-needed 'bottom-up' approach in the area of environmental conservation and linked sustainable development.

In contrast to the situation in China, the NGO sector-based environmental movement in India is well established, contributing towards the decision-making process at all levels. Starting with the efforts made by non-governmental environmental groups and scientific expertise to resist the building of a hydroelectric project in one of the best conserved tropical

27. Yang (2003).

rainforest areas of India i.e., the 'Silent valley' in Kerala,[28] which received international attention too. India can proudly claim to have one of the largest NGO environment-linked sustainable development movement that is comparable with elsewhere in the world. Indeed, this sector has played a crucial role in auditing India's environment from time to time, starting with one of the first 'State of India's Environment' reports published in the early 1980s,[29] with some impact on the governmental decision-making process.

In a larger context, one is concerned with global environmental protection in the 'Kyoto Protocol' framework. With both the countries rapidly trying to catch up with the rest of the developed world, the environmental challenge has to be faced jointly between the developing and the developed world. India and China jointly have a crucial role to play in such an effort. To be effective, environmental conservation, as is amply evident from earlier discussion, has to be a good blend of the 'top-down' planning and development approach with 'bottom-up' community-participatory involvement, which will act as a set of checks and balances, that are mutually supportive of one another. In the ultimate analysis, what one is arguing for is a democratic process that enables diverse sections of society to be involved in a participatory decision-making process, which will enable them to be as close to 'nature' as appropriate. On the one extreme, traditional societies such as forest dwellers are already close to nature, but 'modern' influences have had disruptive influences on them, and this damage needs to be rectified. On the other extreme, those living in a concrete jungle of the urban also, and still have the intrinsic desire to remain as close to nature as possible. In both these extreme situations, the inherent human inclination to remain connected with 'nature', even if that association is somewhat qualitatively different, cannot be underestimated. This attitude towards 'nature' has survived through the ages, even as humans passed through a socio-eco-cultural transformation.[30] For example, even the most modern urban communities of the USA wants to be connected with 'nature' to the extent feasible, through reconstructed 'urban cultural landscapes.[31] In the present India-China regional context, what one is arguing for is to make

28. Ramakrishnan (1984); CSE (1982).

29. CSE (1982).

30. Ramakrishnan (2008a).

31. Shutkin (2000).

a move towards cultural diversity-specific management of natural resources; an opportunity that both India and China should not miss out at this stage, as two are rapidly developing economies.

In the ultimate analysis, knowledge systems-based community participatory approaches, contributing to sustainable economic development is the key to ensure socio-ecological security.[32] With a rich assemblage of ethnic diversity and a large number of minority groups in both the countries, conservation-linked sustainable development has to be based upon a value system that the very diverse sections of society understand and appreciate and in which they feel induce to participate.

References

Agarwal, A. and S. Narain (1997). *Dying Wisdom: Rise and Fall and Potential of India's Traditional Water Harvesting Systems*. New Delhi: Centre for Science & Environment.

Asia Program (2004). "Active Society in Formation: Environmentalism, Labour and the Underworld in China", *Asia Program Special Report*, No. 124, September. Washington DC: Woodrow Wilson International Center for Scholars. p.20.

Bondeau, A., H. Bugmann, B. Campbell, P. Canadell, T. Chapin, W. Cramer, J. Ehleringer, T. Elliott, J. Foley, B. Gardner, J. Goudriaan, P. Gregory, D. Hall, T. Hunt, J. Ingram, C. Korner, J. Landsberg, J. Langridge, B. Lauenroth, R. Leemans, S. Linder, R. McMurtrie, J.C. Menaut, H. Mooney, D. Murdiyarso, I. Noble, B. Parton, L. Pitelka, P.S. Ramakrishnan, O. Sala, B. Scholes, D. Schulze, H. Shugart, M.S. Smith, W. Steffen, B. Sutherst, C. Valentin, B. Walker, I. Woodward and Z.S. Zhang (1997). *The Terrestrial Biosphere and Global Change: Implications for Natural and Managed Ecosystems—A Synthesis of GCTE and Related Research*. (Eds. Walker, B. and Steffen, W). The International Geosphere-Biosphere Programme (IGBP), Stockholm, Sweden. p.32.

Brown, R.L., C. Flavin and H. French (1999). *State of the World*. New York & London: W.W. Norton and Company.

CSE (1982). *The State of India's Environment, 1982: A Citizen's Report*. New Delhi: Centre for Science & Environment. p.189.

Chadha, K.L. and M.S. Swaminathan (eds.) (2006). *Environment and Agriculture*. New Delhi: Malhotra Publishers. p.900.

Dragun, A.K. and C. Tisdell (1999). *Sustainable Agriculture and Environment: Globalisation and the Impact of Trade Liberalisation*. Cheltenham, U.K.: Edward Elgar. p.308.

Economy, Elizabeth (2004). *The Case of China and The Global Environment: Dizzying Growth, Devolution of Power, Environmental Disaster.*

Information Office of the State Council of the People's Republic of China (2006). *Environmental Protection in China (1996-2005)*. June. Beijing.

Kothyari, B.P., K.S. Rao, K.G. Saxena, T. Kumar, P.S. Ramakrishnan (1991). "Institutional Approaches in Development and Transfer of Water-Harvest Technology in the

32. Ramakrishnan (2008b).

Himalaya", in G. Tsakiris (ed.). *Advances in Water Resource Technology*. pp.673-78. A. Balkerma, Rotterdam, Holland.

Ministry of Environment & Forests (1999). *National Forestry Action Programme*. Govt. of India, New Delhi. p.177.

Parrotta, J.A., L. Jinlong and S. Heok-Choh (2008). *Sustainable Forest Management and Poverty Alleviation: Roles of Traditional Forest-related Knowledge*. IUFRO, Vienna, Austria. p.223.

Ramakrishnan, P.S. (2008a). *The Cultural Cradle of Biodiversity*. National Book Trust, New Delhi. p.243.

————. (2008b). "Linking Knowledge Systems for Socio-ecological Security", in Hans Brauch Günter; John Grin; Czeslaw Mesjasz; Heinz Krummenacher; Navnita Chadha Behera; Béchir Chourou; Ursula Oswald Spring; Patricia Kameri-Mbote (eds.), *Facing Global Environmental Change: Environmental, Human, Energy, Food, Health and Water Security Concepts. Peace Research and European Security Studies*. Vol. 2. AFES Press, Germany (in press)

————. (2001). *Ecology and Sustainable Development*. National Book Trust of India, Govt. of India. p.198.

————. (1996). "Conserving the Sacred: From Species to Landscapes", *Nature & Resorces* 32: 11-19. UNESCO.

————. (1993). *Science and its Shortcomings in Environmental Management: The Social Angle*. N. Polunin and J. Burnett (eds.) *Surviving with the Biosphere*. pp.209-32. Edinburgh University Press, Edinburgh.

————. (1992a). *Shifting Agriculture and Sustainable Development: An Interdisciplinary Study from North-Eastern India*. Man and Biosphere Book Ser. 10, UNESCO, Paris and Parthenon Publishers, Caernforth, Lancs, U.K. p.424 (Republished by Oxford University Press, New Delhi. p.424, 1993).

————. (1992b). "Tropical Forests: Exploitation, Conservation and Management", Special issue on *Environment and Development Impact* 42: 149-62. (UNESCO).

————. (1984). "The Need to Conserve Silent Valley and Tropical Rain Forest Ecosystems in India", *Environment Conservation* 11: 170-71.

Ramakrishnan, P.S., K.G. Saxena and K.S. Rao (2006). *Shifting Agriculture and Sustainable Development of North-East India: Tradition in Transition*. UNESCO and Oxford & IBH, New Delhi. p.495.

Ramakrishnan, P.S., K.G. Saxena and U. Chandrasekhara (1998). *Conserving the Sacred: For Biodiversity Management* (UNESCO Vol.). Oxford & IBH, New Delhi. p.480.

Ramakrishnan, P.S., R. Boojh, K.G. Saxena, U.M. Chandrashekara, D. Depommier, S. Patnaik, O.P. Toky, A.K. Gangawar and R. Gangwar (2005). One Sun, Two Worlds: An Ecological Journey. UNESCO and Oxford & IBH, New Delhi. p.286.

Senapati, B.K., S. Naik, P. Lavelle and P.S. Ramakrishnan (2002). "Earthworm-based Technology Application for Status Assessment and Management of Traditional Agroforestry Systems. In P.S. Ramakrishnan, R.K. Rai and R.P.S. Katwal and S. Mehndiratta (eds.), *Traditional Ecological Knowledge for Managing Biosphere Reserves in South and Central Asia*. pp.139-60. UNESCO and Oxford IBH, New Delhi.

Shutkin, W.A. (2000). *The Land that Could Be: Environmentalism and Democracy in the Twenty-First Century*. USA: The MIT Press. p.273.

CCICED (2003). *Summary Report of the Task Force on Financial Mechanism for Environmental Protection, the Third Phase of CCICED, 2003.* Also, *Recommendations to Promote the Development of Chinese Environmental Protection Industry (EPI)*, Draft version, July 27, 2003.

Wenhua, Li (2001). *Agro-Ecological Farming Systems in China*. UNESCO-MAB Vol. Series 26, Carnforth, Lancs: Parthenon Publishers. p.433.

Wolman, M.G., P.S. Ramakrishnan, P.S. George, S. Kulkarni, P.S. Vashishtha, Z. Shidong, Z. Qiguo, Z. Yi, J.F. Long, C. Rosenzweig, W.D. Solecki (2001). *Growing Populations, Changing Landscapes: Studies From India, China and the United States*. (Indian National Science Academy, Chinese Academy of Sciences and the U.S. National Academy of Sciences Publication), Washington DC. USA: National Academy Press. p.299.

Yancheva, G., N.R. Nowaczyk, J. Mingram, P. Peter Dulski, G. Schettler, J.F.W. Negendank, J. Liu, D.M. Sigman, L.C. Peterson and G.H. Haug (2007). Influence of the Intertropical Convergence Zone on the East Asian Monsoon", *Nature* 445: 474-77.

Yang, Guobin (2003). Weaving a Green Web: The Internet and Environmental Activism in China", *China Environment Series* 6, Washington, DC: Woodrow Wilson Centre. pp.89-92.

5 The Internal Political Situation in China

B. Raman

An editorial published on October 15, 2010, by the Communist Party-controlled *Global Times* said: 'China has changed a lot. In the future it will continue to adopt gradualism to bring about changes. No force can compel the nation to change what cannot be changed at the moment... The Chinese cherish stability. They don't want to let a radical revolution overwhelm current reforms. In respect to reforming the political system, China needs political wisdom and constant drive. It doesn't need to rush its forces.'

This editorial was published on the eve of the four-day Fifth Plenary Session of the 17th Central Committee of the Chinese Communist Party, which was held at Beijing from October 15 to 18, 2010. Even though the main item on the agenda of the session was the approval of the next (12th) Five-Year Plan, there was considerable speculation in China and abroad that the session might set in motion a programme of political reforms as a follow-up to the economic reforms launched by Deng Xiaoping in 1978 and the administrative reforms that followed in 1982.

The gradual introduction of a free market economy and the equally gradual integration of the Chinese economy with the global economy were the two pillars of the economic reforms proposed. Deng believed that while a Centrally controlled economy was necessary during a period of revolutionary war, the continuance of the planned economy after the revolutionary war was over, would stand in the way of China's rise as an economic power. His administrative reforms consisted of streamlining the structure of the Government by reducing the number of ministries from about a 100 to 61 and providing a fixed tenure for all holders of political office.

Deng believed that economic reforms, even if successful, would not be sustainable unless they were built on a carefully constructed foundation of political reforms. In a talk on 'The Reform of the Chinese Political System' to the Europe-China Forum in Ireland on September 5, 2003, Prof Liu Ji, Executive President, China Europe International Business School (CEIBS), said as follows: 'As China has now adopted a market-based economic system, great changes have to be made to its superstructure, including its political system. Mr Deng once hit the nail on the head when he stated that without political reform, the economic reform would remain purely superficial, and might even turn out to be a failure.'

Has the time come for launching an ambitious programme of political reforms? If so, what should be the nature of the political reforms to be introduced? What should be the role of the Communist Party in future? These are some of the questions, which were engaging the attention of the political leadership since the 17th National Congress of the Communist Party of China held in October 2007. The debate in the party and in the intellectual circles outside the party focussed on the following points:

> The time has come to undertake changes in the political structure, but such changes should not affect the continuity of the functioning of the State and the Party.
>
> - The Party will be the innovator and the driving force of the political re-structuring as it was of the economic re-structuring after 1978.
> - The individual freedom of speech will be freedom to criticise constructively and not freedom to promote destabilising dissidence.
> - The introduction of political reforms will be gradual just as the introduction of the economic reforms were.

The report presented by President Hu Jintao, in his capacity as the Party Secretary, to the Congress contained 60 references to the expression 'people's democracy'. This expression also figured repeatedly in the subsequent discussion on the report. Both Deng and Jiang Zemin had spoken of socialist democracy as the basis of the proposed political reforms. To quote Prof Liu Ji: 'Mr. Deng pointed out that "socialism is not able to survive without democracy", and it is our mission to "build a socialist democratic political system". Mr Jiang stated that 'we are going to build up a nation based on a socialist democratic political system and the rule of law.' Thus, Hu and Prime Minister Wen Jiabao spoke of people's democracy as well as socialist democracy.

For China's progress and stability in the future, political development was as important as economic and social development. That was what Hu sought to underline in his report. What should be the political characteristics of the Chinese state would be decided by the Chinese people through their Party in accordance with their genius and experience. It would not be imposed from outside. The Chinese media quoted Yang Guangbin,[1] Professor of the Renmin University of China. as saying: 'With more individual freedom, gradual shaping of the unique concept of democracy and the solid forming of institutional arrangements, a China-style democracy is emerging.'

Hu drew attention to the following aspects of democracy in Chinese colours: the supremacy of the Constitution and the rule of the law, avoidance of arbitrariness in decision-making and governance, collective leadership through the Party tempered by a division of individual responsibilities, democratic centralism moderated by inner party democracy, decisions based on information and intellectual support to the decision-making process, self-management, self-service, self-education and self-oversight. He emphasised that 'power must be exercised in the sunshine to ensure that it is exercised correctly'.

During the Congress, the Chinese Party leaders sought to convey to their own people and to the rest of the world that what one saw in China was not the rule of the few over the many, but the rule of the many through the few. They projected China as a state where decisions were made and power was exercised not in darkness, but in full 'sunshine'.

It was stated during the discussion on Hu's report that while China would continue to be a one-party state, the Party should avoid any pretensions to a monopoly of wisdom. Non-Party intellectuals and technocrats would have an increasing role in policy formulation and governance. One need not to be a Party member in order to be associated with the Government, but those associated with the Government—whether they were Party members or not—must accept Party supervision over their functioning.

---

1. Cited in "Democracy: Outstanding Catchphrase in Hu's Keynote Report to CPC Congress", Xinhua, 16 October, 2007. Available at: *http://english.people.com.cn/90002/92169/ 92188/6283724.html*

Liberal democracy has two important features: the right of the people to elect their leaders and to question in open the wisdom of the decisions taken by the Government. Chinese-style democracy would not have these features. The leaders would be elected by the Party cadres in accordance with Party procedures. While there would be a widest possible public contribution to decision-making by the leadership, once a decision was made, its wisdom cannot be challenged. The expression of any reservations or dissent should be in the darkness of Party corridors and not in open sunshine. However, it was stated that the Party had decided to experiment with direct elections of Party chiefs in more than 200 townships in Chongqing, Sichuan and Hubei.

Among those who expressed themselves in favour of political restructuring was Prime Minister Wen Jiabao who himself told the National People's Congress (NPC) on March 5, 2010, while delivering the annual report on the work of his Government: 'China's modernization drive and economic reforms could risk a failure without political restructuring. The Government would create conditions for the people to criticize and supervise the Government, and let news media fully play their oversight role so as to put the authorities under sunlight.'

This debate was further taken forward during functions held in Shenzhen in August-September, 2010, to mark the 30th anniversary of the setting up of the special economic zone (SEZ) under the directive of Deng. In a speech delivered by him at Shenzhen on August 21, 2010, Wen, according to the Xinhua news agency, made the following points: China has to pursue political reform to safeguard its economic health. 'Without the safeguarding of political restructuring, China may lose what it has already achieved through economic restructuring and the targets of its modernization drive might not be reached. People's democratic rights and legitimate rights must be guaranteed. People should be mobilized and organized to deal with, in accordance with the law, state, economic, social and cultural affairs.' Wen also wanted to 'create conditions' to allow the people to criticise and supervise the government as a way to address 'the problem of over-concentration of power with ineffective supervision.'

In an article published on August 23, the *Global Times* commented on Wen's speech as follows: 'Wen's remarks about political reform came 30 years after the late Chinese leader Deng Xiaoping first raised the issue during an important speech on August 18, 1980, which was regarded as "the programmatic document for China's political restructuring." After three decades of reform and opening-up, China is expected to overtake Japan to become the world's second largest economy this year, but the country is facing mounting pressure during its social transition including frequent attacks on vulnerable groups, aggravating pollution, serious corruption, inequality of distribution and a widening income gap. Mounting social unrest in recent years have proved costly. In 2009, the government earmarked 514 billion yuan ($76 billion) to maintain stability, much more than the 480 billion yuan for national defense.'

The article added: 'Zhang Liangui, a professor at the Party School of the CPC Central Committee, noted that the root cause of growing social conflict is the slow pace of political reform that seriously lags behind unprecedented economic reform.' Mao Shoulong, a professor of administrative management at Renmin University, said that we will 'cross the river by touching each stone' during political reform, just like economic reform in the past 30 years, and it should be carried out under the framework of the current political system, which is dominated by the CPC. Democracy would probably be promoted at the grassroot level, especially with the election of lower-ranking officials, Mao added.

The message from the article was clear: yes, China must embark on political reforms, but they should be carried out under the leadership of the Communist Party. The measures undertaken should reform the functioning of the Government and the Party without weakening them.

In his speech at Shenzhen on September 6, Hu Jintao avoided the use of expressions such as political restructuring etc. Hu's emphasis was on Shenzhen as a trigger for the Chinese economic miracle. But Hu's speech was not devoid of references to the political system as made out by some analysts. He said that the SEZs could experiment with reforms in economic, political, cultural and social systems. Hu called for 'expanding socialist democracy' and speeding up the construction of 'a socialist country under the rule of law.' He said efforts should be made to carry out democratic elections, decision-making, management and supervision in order to safeguard the people's right to know, to participate, to express and to supervise.

In September 2010, while he was in New York to attend the UN General Assembly session. Premier Wen Jiabao was interviewed by Fareed Zakaria for CNN's Global Public Square programme. Zakaria asked him about freedom in China: 'Can you be as strong and creative a nation with so many restrictions on freedom of expression, with the internet being censored?' Wen replied: 'I believe freedom of speech is indispensable, for any country, a country in the course of development and a country that has become strong. Freedom of speech has been incorporated into the Chinese constitution. I often say that we should not only let people have the freedom of speech, we more importantly must create conditions to let them criticise the work of the government. It is only when there is the supervision and critical oversight from the people that the government will be in a position to do an even better job, and employees of government departments will be the true public servants of the people.'

From Hu's comments at Shenzhen and from Wen's subsequent interview on the CNN, many analysts jumped to the conclusion that Hu and Wen were probably not on the same wavelength as regards the need for political restructuring in China and greater respect for the freedom of speech. But if one read and analysed carefully the statements and comments made by Hu and Wen since the 17th National Congress of the Party in October 2007, it was evident that in their own respective style both leaders were reflecting the Party line on the need for political restructuring and how to go about it.

However, expectations and speculation that the fifth plenum of the 17th Central Committee would come out with a slew of political reforms as forward-looking and as significant as the economic reforms of the post-1978 years were belied. The advocates of political gradualism and opponents of hasty actions seemed to have prevailed over those advocating a faster pace of political reforms. A communiqué issued at the end of the plenum said that the leadership of the Communist Party of China (CPC) would be the 'fundamental guarantee' for China to achieve the goals of the economic and social development plan for the next five years. It added that steps to improve the CPC's ruling capacity and maintain the Party's advanced nature should be strengthened to promote the Party's competence in leading the country's economic and social development. A reformed, people-friendly

Communist Party and not a reformed political structure has emerged as the present objective.

Why this cautious line? Why, after the enthusiastic debate in the months after October 2007 on the need for political restructuring, the present emphasis on the need for a more gradual approach? Maintaining political stability, economic prosperity and social harmony is the driving force of Chinese policymaking. Three events since October 2007 have made the Chinese leadership feel that they cannot take the present state of stability, prosperity and harmony for granted. Indeed, potentially destabilising factors continue to confront the leadership.

These are: firstly, the economic meltdown; second, the uprising in Tibet in 2008 just before the Olympics; and third, the violent incidents in Xinjiang Province before the Olympics, which were followed by a violent uprising by the Uighurs in the middle of 2009. The economic meltdown resulted in the retrenchment of about 30 million Chinese workers due to the closure of a number of manufacturing industries in the coastal areas due to a drop in orders from the West, particularly the US. These workers had migrated to the coastal areas from the rural areas to take up jobs. Their retrenchment and return to their villages created fears of possible widespread social unrest. However, these fears have been belied, but a new cause of unrest has arisen as a result of the economic re-restructuring undertaken by the Chinese leadership to reduce the dependence on exports and to increase the domestic demand for manufactured goods by increasing the minimum wages of workers in many towns. There have been many instances of workers being dissatisfied with the increase in minimum wages, and resorting to strikes—particularly in foreign-owned enterprises—in order to demand more. Fortunately, such labour unrest has not so far affected Government servants. There have been no reported instances of their resorting to strikes in order to demand an increase in their salaries. If they do so, the political leadership could be faced with a tricky situation. The ambitious stimulus package to keep the economy doing well at a GDP growth rate of eight per cent plus and the increase in minimum wages have led to a spiralling inflationary situation with a potential for social unrest. While dealing with these problems through energetic economic management measures, the Government is at the same time avoiding hasty political actions which could cause instability due to a mix of political and economic factors.

The uprisings in Tibet and Xinjiang jolted the self-confidence of the political leadership which had convinced itself that through economic development it had won the loyalty of the Tibetan Buddhists and the Uighur Muslims. It realised that this was not so. Anti-Han feeling continues to be as high as ever in the Tibetan and Uighur-inhabited areas. Even more than the Uighur uprising of July 2009, what shocked the Government was the anger of the Hans who protested in the streets of Urumqi over the failure of the local government to protect them from attacks by the Uighurs. The danger of the Hans taking the law into their own hands and indulging in a large-scale massacre of the Uighurs, thereby damaging China's relations with the Islamic world, led to Hu Jintao, who had gone to Italy to participate in the G-20 summit, cancelling his participation and returning prematurely to Beijing to chair a meeting of the Central Military Commission to order the dispatch of army units to Xinjiang to help the local police in the restoration of law and order. In Tibet, the Army was not called in to help the civilian authorities in restoring law and order, but in Xinjiang the Army had to be called in.

Maintaining internal security against economic unrest in the Han-inhabited coastal areas and against ethnic unrest in the Tibetan and Uighur inhabited border areas has become a major concern. Chinese leaders have, of late, been speaking of their 'core interests' and 'major concerns'. When they talk of their 'core interests', they mean their disputes with other countries. In their perception, the threats to their core interests arise from abroad. When they talk 'of major concerns', they largely mean threats to their internal security.

While the Chinese authorities have striven to ensure that the rest of the world does not get to know much about the internal security situation, it is in fact a major concern to the leadership. This would be obvious from the enormous budgetary allocation for their internal security apparatus, which, according to the *Global Times* of August 23, 2010 amounts to US $76 billion. If the *Global Times* is to be believed, China spends more money for maintaining political stability than for protecting the country from external threats. Under these circumstances, it is not surprising that the leadership is going slow on political reforms.

Can China disintegrate under the weight of its internal security problems? This is unlikely. The very credible economic prosperity China has achieved and the interest of the homogeneous Han majority as a whole in ensuring that this prosperity is a solid guarantee against any tendency towards disintegration in the Han core of the country. At the same time, the Tibetan and Uighur uprisings have shown that economic prosperity has not diluted yearnings for freedom. So long as this remains alive, the danger of instability in the border areas will remain.

The Chinese leadership has not learnt the right lessons from the Tibetan and Uighur uprisings. It continues to believe that by pumping more money into these areas for bringing their economic development on par with that in the coastal areas, it could dilute separatist tendencies and reduce the feelings of alienation. It is confident that after the death of His Holiness the Dalai Lama, the situation in Tibet will become manageable even if they have to face a short spell of controllable violence. It is also counting on Pakistan and Turkey to help it maintain peace in Xinjiang. At the same time it has taken measures to dilute the ethnic identity of the Tibetans and the Uighurs by making Mandarin the medium of instruction in the Tibetan and Uighur schools. The importance of the Tibetan and Uighur languages has been reduced by making them only second languages. These actions have already evoked fresh protests among the youth and their teachers. However, the protests have remained peaceful. Some of the actions taken by it as mid-course corrections of its policies in the border areas might turn out to be new seeds of fresh unrest.

It is important for India to keep the hopes of the Tibetan youth alive. Indian silence on the developments in Tibet is already causing demoralisation among the Tibetan youth. This policy and our maintaining a distance from His Holiness the Dalai Lama is suiting the interests of the Chinese leadership rather than ours. Thus, we need to be more articulate on Tibet.

6 Whither China: Prospects and Direction?

A Net Assessment of the Social, Cultural and Human Dimensions of China's Development

Ravi Bhoothalingam

This paper is an exercise directed to working out a net assessment of the social, cultural and human factors influencing China's progress towards its stated goals. Any attempt to compress such a broad vista into a few pages of text must necessarily be prefaced with a note expressing humility and caution. The paper is set in six sections, although by the very nature of the topic, there can be no neat compartmentalisation. Section I spells out the broad goals that China has set for itself. The next three sections cover demography (including women's roles and urbanisation), health, migration and minorities. Section V looks at education and aspects of Chinese culture. Each section concludes with some implications for further discussion and analysis. Finally, the closing section attempts a summary of the main conclusions and an assessment of the overall implications for India and the world.

China's Goals

In October 2006, at the sixth Plenum of the Chinese Communist Party's Central Committee, China unveiled its vision to build 'a harmonious society' by the year 2020. According to China's Premier, Wen Jiabao, key features of such a society would be 'achieving a moderate level of prosperity' as well as 'democracy, rule of law, equity, justice, sincerity, amity and vitality....' The long list of goals concludes with 'guaranteeing respect for people's rights and interests...the ecological environment visibly improved, further progress in fostering a sound moral atmosphere and harmonious interpersonal relationships, enhanced creativity of society as a whole and the development of an innovation-based nation'.[1]

This is certainly an ambitious and daunting set of targets for a country that just over 50 years ago suffered a devastating famine and had emerged barely a decade before that from a 100 years of civil war, occupation and semi-colonial rule. How do the prospects look?

Demography

By 2020, China's population will be around 1.4 billion. But more importantly, that 'China will grow old before it becomes rich' is the oft-quoted and stark statement that defines China's predicament—unique amongst developing nations. The number of aged (>64 years) will be 24 per cent in 2050 as against 8 per cent in 2005. The dependency ratio—i.e. children (<15 years) plus 'aged' as a proportion of the population—will rise from 50 per cent to 64 per cent in this period, with a decline in fertility ratios. China will have a 3-generational inverted-pyramid (4-2-1) family structure with its consequent issues and anxieties. How will China cope?[2]

While the 1-child policy (applicable to about 36% of the population holding an urban *hukou*) has yet to be formally amended, it is in practice not as rigid as popularly imagined. For example, Shanghai has already relaxed its rules to permit 2 children. The rural population (52.9%) has effectively 1.5 children and the minorities (11.2%) are at 2.4 children. With a rapid fall in the fertility rate, it is expected that there will be a formal announcement to amend China's population policy, but what is holding it up is China's federal structure, where the provinces wield effective control. However, even a change can make a difference only in the long run. The more immediate remedies for the ageing issue comprise two elements: (a) a rapid and planned urbanisation programme, and (b) the application of science and technology.

Urbanisation has already proceeded at an unprecedented pace in China—the urban population increased from 26 per cent to 42 per cent in 15 years up to 2005. Urban conglomerations like Shanghai and

1. China Daily (2006).
2. Zhang Juwei, Institute of Population and Labor Economics, Chinese Academy of Social Sciences.

Chongqing are megacities planned for capacities of over 40 million each, with transportation, urban facilities and environmental envelopes to match. Properly designed urban facilities are deemed friendlier for the elderly on physical, social and environmental considerations, than the traditional practice of leaving the elders in the family village. The Chinese are learning from Japanese research on ageing which (unlike the West) treats the elderly as a resource rather than as a liability. Thus, the elderly are encouraged to keep learning (through senior citizen universities and similar continuing learning programmes), to contribute to family care and solidarity (an Asian as well as a Confucian value), and increasingly to use technology to keep connected and mobile.

China, Japan and Korea are in the forefront of research on prosthetic devices, robots and household automation. Even if the extended family cannot be physically relocated together in terms of limited housing space, its effects can be approximated through better transport and internet connectivity, and a more engaged and community-oriented elderly population. Finally, the impact of cultural values, diet, exercise and training has been such as to infuse a spirit of largely disciplined living (probably through no choice of their own!) on the part of the elderly, most visible through the ubiquitous early-morning *taiqichuan* groups. This could be a cause for the lower incidence of old-age loneliness and depression than in the West.

Joseph Coughlin (2010) has drawn attention with sharp clarity to the point that while China is a late starter in facing the issues of elderly care and lifestyle, this also gives it an opportunity to formulate creative and novel responses. The size of the problem and its ramifications in terms of medicare, food, communication, housing, transport, telemedicine, education etc., means that there are also huge business implications on a global scale that can be responsive to these needs.

'Women hold up half the sky' said Mao, though both China and India, shamefully, lead the world in female foeticide. Approximately 111 million girls in China are 'missing' through a skewed birth rate favouring boys, accentuated by the 1-child policy, according to some accounts. Others dispute these figures, arguing that massive under-reporting of (second) girl children as well as adoption figures belie these statistics. Still, there is no doubt that there are at least 106-108 male births for every 100 female ones. However, for the girl children who are born, life is not bad. The female-to-male ratio for primary school enrollment is 99 per cent, for secondary 100 per cent and tertiary education 95 per cent (compare India: 94%, 80%, and 70% respectively).[3] Female participation in the workforce is at 80 per cent. Goldman concludes that China has about 15 years to exploit the demographic advantages conferred by a literate and young population.

Implications

1. China's unique and complex demographic challenges will severely tax China's resources.
2. However, creative responses to these challenges can create huge business opportunities.
3. A 15-year window means that China will need to exercise undiluted focus on the matter.
4. An ageing/high dependency ratio society is usually increasingly averse to belligerence.
5. High female participation favourably influences social interaction and governance.

Health

Success in facing the demographic issues will depend in large measure on China's health policy, and here the challenges are even greater than those confronted by the USA.

The Chinese publicly-funded and run health care system set up during the Communist years had succeeded in reducing infant mortality from 200 per 1,000 to 34 per 1,000, and increasing life expectancy from 35 to 68 years by 1982.[4] Central government funding was then abruptly reduced by over 50 per cent and the provinces asked to fill the gap through taxation. Since they could not cover the gap, this brought about an unintended 'privatisation', as health care providers sought revenues through market-related health care

3. Goldman Sachs Global Economic Paper, Issue no.164, March 4, 2008, *https://portal.gs.com*
4. Blumenthal and Hsiao (2005).

charges. Just before that, the communes had been disbanded, dismantling the cooperative health care system available to peasants. This double whammy was not all. Since medical insurance was available only to 29 per cent of the population by 1999 (10% in rural areas), with out-of-pocket costs being 58 per cent (against 20 per cent in 1978), the cumulative effect of all these measures meant that public health deteriorated and infant mortality was up again to 39/1,000 by 2002. By then, the situation had started causing serious concern as a public order issue, and the Central authorities decided to introduce basic rural (2003) and urban (2005) medical insurance, with a target to cover 90 per cent of the population by 2010. In 2009, a national plan was launched with an investment of US $10.5 billion to rejig the entire system wholesale and provide universal health care by 2020.

This story is both tragic and ironic. Tragic, because it is an example of how privatisation can go so horribly wrong; ironic, because the post-Mao reformers, in their attempt to undo the '30 per cent bad' attributed to Mao, actually dismantled a major pillar in the edifice that formed a large part of the '70 per cent good' ascribed to him. The untrammeled rigours of the health market also left the 'barefoot doctors' and the hospital system in tatters, subject to corrupt practices and counterfeit drugs (almost 30%). A major reason for low household consumption (and high savings) in China is that common people need to save money for medical exigencies. Thus, a purely domestic problem works to intensify international economic imbalances.

However, there are some positive sides to the picture. The Chinese government is fully seized with the issue and has acted decisively. China has abundant tax revenues and foreign exchange reserves to fund its national health care, and has stepped up its spending on health to 5.5 per cent of GDP. The successes in tackling Severe Acute Respiratory Syndrome (SARS) and avian flu have been cautionary, and have triggered health-service reorganisation and the formation of pandemic early warning systems in the countryside. An attempt has also been made to improve quality and tackle counterfeiting, especially after the notorious milk scandal of 2007, though quality deficiencies (lead in toys, housing construction defects, mine safety) continue to remain public concerns, hence constituting a serious vulnerability. The introduction of a 'pay-as-you-go' pension scheme which provides a base pension of 20 per cent of the final wage drawn to 64 per cent of urban workers (155 million people) is a start towards a comprehensive social security fund which is being built up rapidly, and now totals 130 billion yuan.[5]

Implications

1. The health care issue affects social stability and thus is a vital sign for the Chinese polity.
2. The financial needs of health care and social security together will pose a serious competing demand to other infrastructure spending including military expenditure.
3. A stimulus to health care and social spending as an element of Chinese public consumption is also important from the viewpoint of global economic rebalancing.

Migration and Minorities

We will now briefly look at migration in its four aspects: rural to urban, from the hinterland to the borderlands (and the minority aspects), Chinese emigration and immigration into China:

Rural to Urban

The largest mass movement of population in the world is the ebb and flow of migrant workers from China's countryside into its cities, and back again, following the remorseless logic of economics. The flow is regulated by the long-standing *hukou* permit system, whereby this migrant labour pool enjoys varying degrees of urban entitlements, but those outside its scope (the large majority) are consigned to the category of a 'floating population' with no urban welfare benefits such as the right to settle, use local public schools etc.[6] In short, the *hukou* places urban China effectively out of bounds to nearly 800 million rural citizens of China. Like migrants everywhere, this labour pool performs the most unwanted tasks. They also keep factory wages low (whilst risking quality and safety) and permitting the extraction of surplus in the time-honoured way so eloquently described by Karl Marx!

---

5. Government of China website: "China's Social Security and its Policy", *www.gov.cn*
6. Chan and Buckingham (2008).

No wonder there have been resounding calls over the years for the system to be abolished if not diluted greatly. However, economic logic, the urban dwellers' fears of being swamped by a human wave of migrants, and not least the self-interest of the migrants themselves, have contributed to the system retaining its basic features, though there has been improvement. The *hukou* rules are now administered by local authorities who have specified conditions and extended benefits in line with supply and demand and in response to popular opinion. The condition of migrants therefore varies greatly, with some cities such as Beijing and Shanghai according migrants a reasonable measure of dwelling, educational and welfare rights, whilst in other areas there has been only marginal change. With labour shortages now appearing in the eastern seaboard and in the Pearl River delta, and working conditions being legislated recently along with wage increases, there has been some improvement. Nevertheless, the entire migrant labour/*hukou* issue is carefully monitored by the Communist Party, as a misstep here can lead to massive popular discontent and a risk to 'social stability'.

Hinterlands to Borderland

Almost on par in terms of sensitivity is the issue of migration from the Chinese heartland to the outlying regions such as Tibet and Xinjiang. Here, China faces a Catch-22 situation. If areas such as Tibet, Xinjiang and Inner Mongolia—once largely populated by minority ethnic groups—are to be developed rapidly, they need human skills. These are in short supply in the resident population, and the time-lag to develop them in the normal course would be far too long. Migration of Han skills has been the Chinese solution, and there has indeed been remarkable development in these provinces. But this has generated great resentment particularly amongst ethnic Tibetans and Uighurs, as the fruits of development appear weighed in favour of the better-off Han migrants. It is generally accepted that the Han population in Xinjiang is around 45 per cent of the provincial total, but in Tibet the Han percentage is hotly contested.[7] Since these are sensitive border provinces, the Chinese need to address the issues with speed, imagination and flexibility of response. Particularly ominous for China is Xinjiang's proximity to Central Asia and the adverse reaction of the Muslim world (particularly Turkey) to the Uighur-Han clashes of July 2009.

7. Mackerras (2005).

Emigration from China

The Chinese diaspora throughout the world numbers over 35 million people, but what is less well known is that almost 18 million of them have emigrated out of China after the liberalisation of the late 1970s.[8] With China's concentrated thrust into Africa over the last decade, a new feature has been the movement of large Chinese workforces into the region to execute development projects. This is estimated to number 750,000, of which the bulk are project workers who will return home or move on to another assignment after their term. But there are incipient trends such as the movement of 10,000 farmers from Hebei province,[9] and the natural fit between a China short of arable land and an Africa with few modern agricultural skills could increase the pace of long-term farming migration to Africa.

An intriguing possibility is the Russian Far East, comprising one-third of Russia's area but rapidly depopulating.[10] Current estimates of the Chinese population in Russia range from 200,000 to 400,000, the majority being seasonal shuttle traders between China's northeast and Siberia. The Chinese are very sensitive to popular Russian fears of a 'Yellow Peril' and so will proceed with caution and in tandem with the Russian government. The recent large-scale Sino-Russian agreements to jointly exploit Siberian minerals, natural gas and resources leads one to speculate that there will be greater movement of people sooner rather than later.

Immigration into China

Finally, China itself is for the first time facing immigration issues, *albeit* on a small scale. There is illegal immigration from North Korea, Vietnam and Laos in China's border areas, in response to the demand for cheap farm labour. 10 per cent of the 26 million foreigners in China are looking for jobs.[11] Two lakh foreign students study in China, and there are 152,000 expatriates in Shanghai alone. Driven by the US$100 billion annual bilateral trade between China and Africa, Guangzhou has over 100,000

8. Kwong (2007).
9. The Independent (2008).
10. Abelsky, Paul (2006).
11. Pomfret (2009).

Africans, mostly buyers and traders, giving rise to issues of visa overstaying and racial discrimination. Such problems are new and uncharted waters for the hitherto generally self-contained and homogeneous Chinese people.

Implications

1. Migrant labour reduces labour costs but can disrupt internal stability if mismanaged.
2. Han migration and insensitive development can disturb the peace in Tibet and Xinjiang.
3. With increases both in emigration and immigration, China will have to cope with novel problems such as cultural adjustments and race relations, with international ramifications.
4. The logic of globalisation must ultimately make labour movement freely possible from areas of labour surplus to labour-scarce economies. Both India and China have a common interest in working together for such a change in the global immigration regimes.

Education and Culture

The early Communist regime laid the foundations for a sound educational system in China, and unlike in the case of health, this structure has not been dismantled. Accordingly, China has a good foundation on which she can build for the future. The overall literacy rate is 93 per cent (UNDP, 2009)[12]; enrollment in nine years of compulsory schooling is 95 per cent (out of a 12-year school system). Sexual parity in education, as already described, is very positive. There are 2,236 institutions of higher education with an enrollment of 20 million graduates and postgraduates. Seven lakh Chinese study overseas whilst 200,000 foreigners study in China, excluding another estimated 100,000 doing language courses of various types. Further, 316 'Confucius Institutes' are dotted all over the world, teaching Chinese language and culture to over 100 million people in 94 countries. The target is to establish 1,000 institutes by 2020.

12. Drawn from "Chapter 10: Table 10.1 (Source: World Bank, UNDP and UNESCO reports)", Economic Survey 2009-10, Ministry of Finance, Government of Pakistan.

In order to achieve the goals of 'an innovation-based society', China has embarked on an ambitious 'National Medium and Long-term Talent Development Plan 2010-2020.'[13] This will increase the talent pool from 114 million to 180 million so as to enable China to move up the value chain in manufacturing so as to create more designs and brands. Another focal point is to attract talented human capital (not just financial capital). Out of the 1.62 million graduates who have left China since 1978, only 500,000 (30%) have returned, so this is a priority area. Trends in the last few years have been encouraging with the returnee ratio increasing as also the numbers of overseas Chinese and foreigners wishing to work in China. The Plan also focusses on increasing the supply of talent and skills in critical service areas such as health care, R&D, law, energy, environment, technicians, financial services etc. This means a mindset change towards the service sector and intellectual capital which in turn will create pressures for more open access and communication between China and the world.

The portents for education are positive. Like most other Asian cultures, there is strong social and family support towards education. Investible resources, domestic and foreign, are available, and there is focussed Government action. China's booming economy and job prospects attract talent, and this momentum will grow with candidates from both developing countries and a declining Europe. The crucial trick will lie in how China reconciles the introduction of 'openness' while not threatening Party control or 'social stability'. This calls for a look at China's underlying cultural DNA that permeates all of its politics and society.

One of the remarkable features of the past 15 years in China has been the revival of its age-old ethical and religious traditions—Confucianism, Taoism and Buddhism. Indeed, this has been encouraged by the Chinese Communist Party (CCP) as they consider these belief systems a welcome counterweight to the rampant and unbridled capitalist spirit and dodgy ethical practices prevalent in the Chinese economy under 'market socialism'. The CCP views these traditions as free from any extraterritorial influence—such as the Vatican or the Dalai Lama. Secondly, the Confucian tradition strongly advocates public education, 'self-cultivation' and meritocracy. Finally, in essence, Confucianism is not incompatible with 'socialism with Chinese characteristics'. The concept of 'harmony'—now a staple of

13. Huiyao (2010).

CCP jargon for both domestic and foreign affairs—has always been core to Confucian thought.

These cultural props are vital to bolstering the CCP's legitimacy while it is engaged in the careful balancing act of fulfilling its implicit contract with the Chinese people—to deliver social and economic prosperity in exchange for a partial suspension of their civil and political rights. For this bargain—today's equivalent of the age-old 'Mandate of Heaven'—to succeed, the governing capability of the Party has to match if not exceed the gravity of the challenges facing it. And those challenges—political, economic, social, environmental—are legion. Can the Party—no doubt a formidably self-reflective and learning organisation—deliver?

Scholars such as Kang Xiaoguang (2005) have opined that the way out of China's dilemma will be through a redefinition of democracy in terms of what harmonises with Confucian culture. He considers that China should think of Anglo-American liberal democracy not as the culmination but as a way-station in the evolution of democracy from its Athenian days. Democracy, therefore, can have a Chinese avatar with Chinese characteristics. Bhoothalingam (2010a) has speculated elsewhere that Kang's views, along with those of Daniel Bell (2008) and Jiang Qing (2003), might well culminate in China ultimately emerging as a 'Confucian democracy'.

Chinese society is moving in this direction, though the pathway is anything but smooth. It appears to our eyes to be particularly jerky and fitful because our conception of China's society is of an ordered one which largely follows the prescription set down by an authoritarian Central government. The reality, however, is quite different. There are ongoing turf battles between provincial governments and the Central authority, and policies in different territories can vary markedly. The extent to which, for example, freedom of expression (or more correctly—freedom to publish) exists, is not clearly defined. The very lack of definition makes experimentation possible, and new limits can be tested. These attempts are sometimes successful, sometimes not. Different Party bodies, factions, the PLA formations etc., each articulate slightly different variations. There is thus a somewhat inchoate process in assessing what might be termed a clear current of public opinion, but there is a method in this seemingly opaque process. It allows the Party to test the boundaries of what directions are desirable to follow, (and what others might lead to 'instability') in its constant focus to keep

China on the track of 'growth with social stability'. This process can lead to stressful intervals of seeming chaos, but the overall commonality of interests are likely to ensure that the polity as a whole will not succumb to *luan*—or 'great disorder'—a feared outcome for almost every Chinese citizen.

Despite its achievements, China is a poor advocate for itself and an inexpert communicator of its own dilemmas. Its discourse often appears as stilted and its public diplomacy is largely formulaic. Its understanding of other cultures is inadequate, and its conduct in the face of differences is often to retreat into insularity, and a mentality of 'a walled enclosure'. Nevertheless, in the opinion of most Chinese and Asian observers, the most possible end-point of Chinese socio-polity in the near term is likely to be some form of East Asian type of 'directed democracy'. Although the Chinese constantly caution that their system is not for export and that each nation should work out its own pathway in terms of governance processes, it is likely that going forward, the Chinese and Indian versions of democracy will continue to be compared for effectiveness and efficiency amongst emerging nations, particularly in Africa.

Implications

1. China is on course to achieve its goals in terms of education and skill development.
2. Whether this delivers modernisation (not westernisation) or not depends on the quality and sustainability of China's governance, for which the latter must fit China's cultural matrix.
3. The governance-culture interaction means that China's rise will follow a biological process known as 'punctuated equilibrium'—long progress periods with chaotic 'reset' intervals.
4. China's culture and language have emerged as strong projections of her 'soft power.'
5. China will most probably evolve towards an East Asian pattern of a 'directed democracy', which will evoke interest in African and less developed Asian nations.

Conclusions and Action Ideas

In this paper, a certain selectivity has been unavoidable in the choice of topics covered. It is now time to assemble the conclusions and list some action priorities for India.

Challenges and Focus

In attempting to achieve their stated goals, the Chinese face a formidable number of challenges—development, demography, social security and health, regional imbalances, ethnic insecurities and others not covered in this paper. This will demand focussed attention by China's polity for the next several decades. During this transition, China will simultaneously display features of a great power, a middle-income nation as well as an emerging economy.

China's growth as well as Chinas' challenges offers opportunities for India. There will be business opportunities particularly in IT, pharmaceuticals and health care, education and English teaching, management, consulting and financial services, tourism, entertainment, sports and culture. The Indian and Chinese economies offer many examples of complementarity where synergies and economies are possible if the two parties work together. In other areas, there are potentialities to learn from each others'[14] experience. Such engagement should not await 'a final solution' to the Sino-Indian border question.

Belligerence and Assertiveness

If it is to deliver growth and governance despite these challenges, China's leadership needs to be one step ahead of the curve. The risks of not doing so are far greater for its leadership than for those in any electoral democracy. Moreover, the financial pressures of coping with these challenges will mean that the current rate of military expenditure on modernisation cannot be sustained in the long term. As she develops (and ages), it is therefore unlikely that China will engage intentionally in adventurism or armed conflict. However, as a symptom of 'punctuated equilibrium', China will continue to show signs of erratic and apparently uncoordinated

14. Bhoothalingam (2010b).

behaviour arising out of internal jockeying, perceived statecraft, plainly poor public diplomacy or a combination of all of these.

Understanding and 'reading' China are important skills, and India must move rapidly to build a cohort of people who can understand and (literally) interpret China with depth. Two rising and continental powers cannot engage meaningfully on such an inadequate base of mutual comprehension and knowledge. Sunzi's saying is apt here: 'What enables the wise sovereign...to achieve things beyond the reach of ordinary men...is foreknowledge.'[15]

A failure to do this could well lead to conflict, born not out of intention, but through blunders and blind spots arising out of 'a chain of misperceptions and misunderstandings.'[16]

Regional and Global Engagement

As noted, China exhibits a curious duality of behaviour in its dealings. There is confidence, even arrogance, but also insecurity and a sense of victimhood. This can be understood if one appreciates China's reading of its history of the last 200 years. In terms of opportunity for India, it presents several openings.

Rather than be diffident in regional fora (BCIM, SCO, RIS) which involves China, it is in India's interest to engage more vigourously. There are a number of issues, beyond those already on the table, where there can be congruence with China and which are also in the interest of the common neighbourhood, *viz.*, migration policies, nuclear and conventional arms limitation, educational and professional cross-certifications, tourism policies etc. India's communication and diplomatic skills will certainly enable us to make a contribution.

India should also have a much more vigorous Track 2, commercial and people-to-people exchange with Myanmar, Sri Lanka, Nepal, Bhutan and Bangladesh, and should utilise and leverage in particular its educational assets and soft power to much greater effect.

---

15. Sun Zi, *The Art of War*.
16. Ranganathan and Khanna (2004) used this evocative phrase to express the descent.

References

Abelsky, Paul (2006). "An Exaggerated Invasion", *Russia Profile*, December 10, Refers to an 18 per cent decline.

Bardhan, Pranab (2010). *Awakening Giants, Feet of Clay*. Delhi: Oxford University Press.

Bell, Daniel (2008). *China's New Confucianism*. Princeton University Press.

Bhoothalingam, Ravi (2010a). *China 2020: A Confucian Democracy?*. Mumbai: Observer Research Foundation.

————. (2010b). "Ways of Thinking: Psycholinguistic Reflections on Sino-Indian Relationships and Potentialities", *ORF Discourse* Issue 2, April.

Blumenthal, David and W. Hsiao (2005). "Privatization and its Discontents: The Evolving Chinese Healthcare System", *New England Journal of Medicine* 353, September.

Chan, Kam Wing and Will Buckingham (2008). "Is China Abolishing the Hukou System?", *The China Quarterly* 195.

China Daily (2006). *Report of the Resolution adopted at the 6th Plenum*, October 29.

Coughlin, Joseph (2010). "China's Gray Revolution", *Innovation,* February 21.

Dikotter, Frank (1992). *The Discourse of Race in Modern China*, London: Hurst & Company.

Huiyao, Wang (2010). "Attracting Talent for the Future", *China Daily*, September 14.

Jacques, Martin (2009). *When China Rules the World*, London: Allen Lane.

Kwong, Peter (2007). Chinese Migration Goes Global: Migrants from the World's Most Populous Nation Influence More than 150 Countries", *YaleGlobal*, 17 July. Yale Center for the Study of Globalization.

Mackerras, Colin (2005). "People's Republic of China: A Background Paper on the Situation of the Tibetan Population", United Nations High Commissioner for Refugees, February.

Peerenboom, Randall (2007). *China Modernizes*. New York: Oxford University Press.

Pomfret, James (2009). "Out of Africa into China, Immigrants struggle", *Reuters,* August 21.

Qing, Jiang (2003). Political Confucianism, Beijing (*shenghuo dushu xinshi sanlian shudian*).

Ranganathan, C.V. and Vinod Khanna (2004). *India and China: The Way Ahead*. Har-anand Publications.

The Independent (2008). "China's New Export Farmers", *December* 29.

Xiaoguang, Kang (2005). *The Third Path of China's Political Development*. World Scientific Publishing Pvt. Ltd., Singapore.

---

7 China–US Relations

H.H.S. Viswanathan

Today, the single most important bilateral relationship in the world which has maximum global impact is undoubtedly that between China and the USA. On the one hand, it is not like the relationship of the two superpowers in the Cold War era; on the other, it is not that of two allies. What we actually have is a complex relationship between a rapidly rising power and a slowly declining one. There are elements of cooperation and competition at the same time. A strong mutual dependence is the crux of this relationship. In this symbiotic relationship, as some scholars have called it, one side has been doing the saving while the other has been doing the spending. The complementarities have even prompted people like Moritz Schularick of Berlin's Free University and Niall Ferguson of Harvard to coin the term like 'Chimerica.' Soon after the installation of the Obama administration, Secretary of State Hillary Clinton remarked that US-China relations would be the single most important foreign policy issue for the US in October 2010, she said 'the relationship between China and US is complex and of enormous consequence, and we are committed to getting it right...In the 21st century, it is not in anyone's interest for US and China to see each other as adversaries. So, we are working together to chart a positive, cooperative and comprehensive relationship for this new century—and we do look forward to working closely with China, both bilaterally, and through key institutions as it takes on a greater role and, at the same time, more responsibility in global and international affairs.'

Framework

Keeping in mind the overall theme of the Seminar, this paper has been prepared with the following framework:

1. Objectives and tasks which China has set for itself in shaping its relationship with the USA.

2. Milieu and the international setting in which China is trying to fulfill these objectives and tasks.
3. US' perceptions of the policies and actions of China.
4. China's perceptions of the policies and actions of US.
5. Hurdles to and prospects for greater China-US cooperation, and
6. Implications for India.

Objectives and Tasks

China's paramount overall objective as articulated by its leaders over the last three decades i.e., the post-Mao era, namely to make itself economically strong, to become a middle income country by 2020 and to be a fully developed one by 2040. Earlier sessions of the ORF China Seminar series have gone into these aspects in depth. Following up on the assessments made in the previous China seminars, it would be appropriate to first highlight that China seems to be on the right track for achieving these objectives. In 1990, the Chinese indicated that to achieve this goal, they had to double their GDP every five years and this is precisely what they have done so far. (In 1990 China's GDP was $390 billion and in 2009 it was $5,365 billion.) Nobel Laureate economist Robert Fogel has predicted that by 2040, China's GDP will be $123 trillion i.e., 40 per cent of the global GDP while that of US will shrink to 14 per cent and that of Europe will be 5 per cent. Of course, this achievement of China's economy has been a part of the 'four modernisation' programmes: agriculture, industry, defence and S&T. The unstated sub-text in this is China's ambition to be a global power, playing an important role in determining the global agenda and shaping the political and economic architecture of the world. China is keen to rapidly increase its comprehensive national power (CNP), a concept formulated by China (*Zonghe guoli*) which is a combination of many factors including soft power.

Milieu and the International Setting

The world has changed, in some ways dramatically, from the time China set the above goals for itself. A good reference point for looking at the international setting would be the end of the Cold War. It would be useful to flag some major developments in the post-Cold War period which have had a defining influence on China's relations with US.

Soon after the end of the Cold War and well into the 1990s the Chinese formulation on the international scene was 'the old order has ended and a new one is yet to take shape.' The unsaid part was, of course, China's desire to seize the opportunity to be a major player in the new order. However, since they were economically and militarily not powerful enough, they had to bide their time. They had also just come out of the Tiananmen tragedy and were isolated internationally and had to wait for a change the mood of the 'international community'.

Two important lessons that China learned from the Cold War was, first, not to get into a disastrous arms race with the US and second not to let political reforms get out of control—the two errors committed by the USSR.

The next event to influence their thinking was the Gulf War of 1991. China woke up to the power of US' high technology weapons which decimated the Iraqi army—the fourth largest standing army in the world at that time—in a matter of days. This led to the reorganisation of PLA—fewer soldiers, more hi-tech weapons, formulation of new military doctrines, investments in the Navy etc. This was a military modernisation that went beyond the contours envisaged by Deng Xiaoping in the early 1980s.

The Taiwan crisis of 1995-96 was a very significant episode in the evolution of China-US ties. President Clinton agreed on a visit to the US by the Taiwan President; China saw it as affecting its core interests. In an aggressive reaction, China fired missiles (without warheads, of course) landing them close to Taiwan's shores. The US dispatched two aircraft carriers and 20 warships. Eventually the situation was de-escalated, and the October 1997 Agreement called for a 'constructive strategic partnership.'

NATO expansion into the former Warsaw Pact countries was seen by China as a blatant attempt by US to take maximum advantage of its poster as the sole superpower and penetrate new areas.

The next development relating to the US, which was noted with considerable concern in Beijing was the formation in 1997 of the neo-conservative think tank, 'Project for the New American Century (PNAC)'.

The policy document of this think tank entitled 'rebuilding America's defences' openly advocated total global military domination. The fact that many of the people associated with this organisation rose to very important positions in the Bush administration (Elliot Abrams, John Bolton, Dick Cheney, Donald Rumsfeld, Paul Wolfowitz and Robert Bruce Zoellick, to name a few), was seen by China as a prelude to a more aggressive US. As expected, Bush did not continue the 'constructive strategic partnership' but referred to China as 'a potential peer competitor'.

Earlier there was also the incident of the bombing of the Chinese Embassy in Belgrade on May 7, 1999 in which three Chinese nationals were killed. China perceived this as a grave provocation. Jiang Zemin refused to take Clinton's calls. There were massive demonstrations (some orchestrated by the Chinese government, no doubt) outside the US Embassy and the Consulates in China. Clinton and Jiang finally spoke a week later to bring down tensions.

The 9/11 tragedy in the US elicited sympathy from China; however, the subsequent war on terror caused anxiety in Beijing, which saw this as an attempt, by the US to using the opportunity to encroach into the Central Asian Republics. These regions are of strategic interest to China, and US was getting too close for comfort.

The next important development was the Iraq War of 2003. For China it was both a lesson as well as an opportunity to be exploited. Ironically China was the President of the UNSC when Resolution 1441 on Iraq was adopted, despite strong reservations from China, France and Russia. They could not stop the attack; they were only able to water down the Resolution by ensuring that it did not directly authorise war. The opportunity for China from this was to exploit US-Europe difference of views on the issue. China also observed that US was not able to punish France and Germany for their open opposition to the war. Was this not a decline in US influence in Europe? Hu Jintao's subsequent visits to Europe, Africa and Latin America in the aftermath fully exploited the skcepticism of many countries on US policies.

The new aggressive diplomacy of China in the 2004-2007 period seems to be a game changer. In January 2007, China shot down a space satellite with a missile; this was clearly meant to be as a 'technology demonstration' to the world. In the same month China vetoed a UNSC Resolution on Myanmar's human rights. This was China's first veto since 1997.

The last important development affecting China-US relations was the financial crisis of 2008 and the consequent recession. US dependence on China increased further because of this development. China managed to come out of the crisis as a responsible global player in the recovery process by implementing a quick and substantial stimulus package.

While taking the above developments as factors which have influenced China's policy towards the US, it should also be noted that throughout the period, China's trade with US and American FDIs into China grew exponentially. This was also the period when China started investing its huge trade surplus which has reached a figure of over US $1 trillion by 2010 in US Treasury bonds and other US instruments.

US' Perceptions of the Policies and Actions of China

China's rise has increased its ability to challenge US' role in the Asia-Pacific region and eventually in other areas. Even though there has been no confrontation, US is fully aware of China's power projection on the basis of its 'core interests.' The recent aggressive behaviour of China in the South China Sea has been noted by the US as a deliberate move in a long-term strategy. The space satellite technology demonstration (2007) mentioned above and the building of a massive sub-terranean naval base in Hainan were also seen as a significant development in China's military capability, not fully in consonance with a 'peaceful rise.' Strategic thinkers in the US are of the view that the long-term objective of Chinese Navy is to operate beyond the 'first island chain' (a line from Japan through Okinawa to Taiwan and south to Philippines) to the 'second island chain' (a line from Japan southward past Guam to Australia), in effect dominating half of the Pacific.

The US is also keenly observing the internal contradictions in China—the growing inequalities, dissatisfaction among migrant labour, increasing incidents of labour unrest and growing corruption. On the question of political reforms, most American analysts see the realistic picture that a Tiananmen-type uprising is highly unlikely in the near future. China has, so far, handled the thousands of labour protests fairly successfully by isolating them and giving them a purely economic connotation rather than making them political. At the same time, China has also been experimenting with some political reforms at the village level. There is also more debate within the Party; however, a Western type multiparty democracy is not likely to emerge for a long time.

S&T is an area where China is catching up fast, but the US knows that it is far ahead. Recently the National University of Defense Technology in Tianjin developed Tianhe-1A, the fastest supercomputer in the world overtaking the existing American models. Nonetheless, it is not as though such achievements have been registered across the entire spectrum of S&T. The US is still home to more than half of the world's top 500 supercomputers. China's global 'high-tech' exports are in the range of $250 billion, i.e., one-third of its total exports. However, 91 per cent of the advanced tech products (ATP) are communication-related products and further most of them are assembled from imported parts and components.

US' indebtedness to China is the most written about subject now-a-days. It is a problem which does not have an immediate solution. US' vulnerability on this score should not be exaggerated, for it is not in China's interest to suddenly change its holdings into other currencies lest the value of its own assets should drop drastically.

China's obsession with energy security is an area of potential conflict. Here again the US is aware of the internal debate in China. There is a growing feeling that Chinese foreign policy has been hijacked by the petroleum lobby, particularly by the China National Petroleum Corporation (CNPC) and the China National Offshore Oil Corporation (CNOOC). By bowing to their pressure, China has been made to look rather irresponsible on the global scene because of support for regimes in places like Sudan and Myanmar. Connected with its obsession with energy security is China's effort to establish a significant presence in the Indian Ocean. The security of the Malacca Straits, through which 80 per cent of China's oil imports pass is an area of concern for China. For their part, US analysts seem to be worried about in the first place, is how aggressively will China move into the Indian Ocean.

The recent 'indigeneous innovation' drive by the Chinese government has, according to US companies, denied a level-playing field. Chinese state owned firms are being favoured for financial incentives and even for mergers and acquisitions putting western enterprises at a disadvantage. This, in the views of many, is counterproductive, since China is alienating its strongest lobby in the US, namely big business.

It is on the international scene that US has very serious doubts on China's actions. Since the mid-1990s, China's diplomatic moves in ASEAN has yielded beneficial results. China's role in the 1997 East Asian financial crisis, when it refused to devalue its currency and took measures to help out the ASEAN countries was seen as a leadership act in the region. It is clear to the US that China wants to achieve regional primacy as the foundation for laying bigger claims on the global scene. The Free Trade Agreement between China and ASEAN in 2004, in US' perception, is an attempt to shift the decision-making centre of the region to Beijing. The formation of ASEAN+3 and China's initial attempts to keep the US out of the East Asia Summit are also seen in the same light. China's rejection of the US proposal for a comprehensive Pacific Rim Free Trade Zone under the APEC framework is another example. US is also apprehensive of the increasing influence of Shanghai Cooperation Organisation (SCO) and its attempts to deny a major US role in the strategic region of Central Asia by China and Russia.

The 'go-global' strategy of China's national champions of industry and the creation of a $200 billion Sovereign Wealth Fund for investments abroad is causing considerable concern in US, which, in a critical analysis of this, has called for an agreed framework for rules on foreign investments. China finds this approach is in contradiction to free market principles.

The constant refrain of US these days is that China is not taking on more global responsibilities. American critics feel that while China has benefitted enormously from the existing world order, it is not lending the system sufficient support commensurate with its power, to strengthen what the Americans call a 'rule-based conduct of international relations.' The indication that China does not attach the desired importance to what the US considers the four most critical global issues (global economic crisis, terrorism, climate change and nuclear proliferation) is an irritant for the US. There is a serious dichotomy here: while US asks 'is China ready to take on more global responsibilities', China asks 'is the US willing to share global power.'

The other major concern of US is the growing 'soft power' projection of China. China's model of national growth has elicited admiration in many countries. With the Washington Consensus based on liberal democracy and capitalism having suffered a serious setback, there has even been talk of a 'Beijing Consensus' (a term coined by the American consultant Joshua Cooper Ramo). It is another matter that for their own reasons the Chinese were not keen to play this concept.

The debates in US on China dwell either on engagement or on containment. There was even a new term coined for the purpose—'congagement.' Given the systems of pressure groups and lobbies working in the US, the debate on China gets to be exaggerated on both sides by the 'engagers' as well as by the 'containers'. The former tend to overestimate the economic opportunities, while the latter tend to overestimate the military threat.

China's Perceptions of the Policies and Actions of US

China is fully aware that as the status quo global power, US will do whatever it takes to slow down its rise. At the most fundamental level, China's biggest fears are US attempts at *fenhua* (splitting the country), and *xihua* (westernise the country). The first is a euphemism for US support to the causes of Taiwan, Tibet and Xinjiang. The second is a euphemism for US promotion of liberal multiparty democracy. These, for the Chinese, are 'core interests' on which there could be no compromise. Hu Jintao emphasised this during Obama's visit to China in November 2009.

China is deeply suspicious of US' actions which, in their view, are aimed at curbing its economic growth. For example while the US complains about the huge trade imbalance, it also restricts or bans the export of high-tech products and technology. This policy help reduce tensions. Proposed Chinese investments in the US also face hurdles. The cases of the takeover bid by CNOOC of Unocal, and that of IBM's PC Division by Lenovo are quoted in this context. China also rejects US' arguments on currency rate manipulations being the main cause for the global economic problem.

The other important economic issue pertains to intellectual property rights (IPR). Since US will rely more and more on IPR for their revenues in the years to come, China sees a trend of US seeking to extend the scope and duration of patents. This has been one of the reasons for the new 'indigeneous innovation' drive in China.

On international issues, China has made it clear that it cannot share US priorities on matters of great concern. Chinese scholars have argued that issues such as Iran's nuclear ambitions, though important, are not crucial for China. From the Chinese perspective, the US sees China as a monolith and fails to see a multiplicity of identities as a developing country, a rising power, a quasi-global power and a socialist state with Chinese characteristics, all at the same time. This wrong perception by the US makes for unreasonable expectations of China.

When the US wants China to play a greater global role, China does not see a corresponding readiness on US' part to share power. China feels that it is being asked to use its influence in promoting a US agenda. This may have been the reason why China did not take up the idea of a G-2 suggested first by Brzezinski before Obama's visit to China. According to them, international governance rules have to evolve with changing circumstances and the US policy of 'one-size-fits-all' model of neoliberal globalisation is not good for the world.

Hurdles to and Prospects for China-US Relations

One of the main hurdles at the conceptual level is the idea of 'US exceptionalism', which assumes that 'its national values and practices are universally valid and this gives US a right, or more accurately a duty to enforce them.' To complicate things, because of its own long history and civilisation, China has its own version of exceptionalism, though on a more modest scale.

The US sponsored principles of 'limited sovereignty' and 'humanitarian intervention' are anathema to Chinese thinking. For them, non-interference in the internal affairs of a country is the foundation of international relations.

Taiwan and Tibet are issues which are bound to flare up from time to time, depending on specific American actions. This was seen after Obama's meeting with Dalai Lama in February 2010. The meeting was originally scheduled in October 2009, but was postponed keeping in view of Obama's pending visit to China in November 2009. Similarly, any future arms sales to Taiwan will create a diplomatic incident. The last such incident was in early 2010 when the Obama administration notified Congress that it planned to sell weapons systems to Taiwan worth US $6.4 billion. In an angry response, China cancelled some military exchange programmes with the US and imposed sanctions against US companies supplying the systems.

Another basic hurdle is the difference in political systems. China may have introduced limited political reforms and might also continue to expand them, but the fact remains that for them society comes first, whereas for the US it is the individual.

On the strategic plane there is deep distrust. This is only to be expected between two major powers, particularly when one is rising and the other appears to the declining. It is not in US interest that China has serious economic or political setbacks. Ideally, US would like a moderately growing China with limited global ambitions. But history shows that with the development of economic and military strength, countries acquire extra-regional interests and the capacity to engage in extra-regional affairs. The mutual distrust, if not handled tactfully, could escalate to dangerous levels as was seen in the stand-off between the US and Chinese navies in March 2009.

For stability, what is needed is a new international understanding and basic rules for trade, use of force, procedures for managing territorial disputes and most importantly mutual recognition of each others' core interests. Unfortunately, we do not see this at present.

China has gained enormously from the current global order. Globalisation has helped China to increase its GDP 14 times over two decades. It is present at all the high tables where decisions of global importance are taken. China would not therefore like to upset the apple cart. Nonetheless, the long-term strategy is to be in a position to change the rules of the game as well as to set its own agenda. In his recent book, *The Frugal Superpower* (2010), Michael Mandelbaum, says that, 'fortunately in the present day world the capacity to change the global order is inversely proportional to the incentive.' He takes three examples: China, Iran and Russia, and goes on to say that China has the maximum capacity and the minimum incentive; Iran has the maximum incentive and the minimum capacity; Russia is somewhere in between. In this exercise of changing the global order, China will, no doubt, co-opt others on an issue-based approach. The Chinese scholar Baohui Zhang (2010) calls this 'soft-balancing.'

The present state of China-US relations has been described as 'cold peace' i.e., stability based on competition and mutual deterrence. If the two sides find more common ground and understanding, this could evolve into a 'warm peace.' i.e., stability based on cooperation and mutual assurance. China Daily used a slightly different term for this kind of stability calling it 'mutually assured dependence.'

Implications for India

How does the complex relationship between China and US affect India? Does India fit in the China-US equation at all and if so, how? Can an adversarial relation between China and US benefit India?

India-US relations today are not in the same league as those between China and the US. The mutual dependence of India and US and traction between the two countries needs to reach much higher levels before we can be there. The US still considers the shared values of democracy, free press, independent judiciary etc., as the most important factor in the strategic partnership. However, India would like the US not to treat this as an end in itself but as a means to an end, namely more affirmation and collaboration in India's acquiring greater economic, technological and political clout.

One should also recognise the asymmetry in the India-China equation. China is a more fraught subject in India than India is in China. This is because of historical reasons as well as unbalance in national strength. The idea of a G-2 between US and China was an unpleasant surprise for India. Though the idea did not get any traction, largely due to Chinese reluctance, doubts about US being a reliable partner could well have been reinforced. The reference to China playing a role in South Asia in the China-US communiqué of 17 November 2009 did considerable damage to building trust and confidence in India.

In the US-China-India triangle, India is the weakest side. For India, in the near future, the conflicts of interests with China will outweigh those with the US. It is therefore natural that India will try to leverage Indo-US relations in its dealings with China. But how far can India go on this path without limiting its autonomous decision-making ability?

Recent US formulations on the triangular US-China-India relations are highly nuanced. They go something like: The US would like to have good relations with China. It would also like India and China to have strong bilateral relations. Now, we see a rising China showing signs of assertiveness and the US, India and others in the region are concerned about this. We hope that China's rise will be peaceful and not threatening to the others in the region. From time to time one hears of 'the China containment' policy of the US. Would the US want India to play a critical role in this? Even if it were so, India would have to take a nuanced position of constructive engagement rather than one of containment.

Recent history has shown that India's attempt at leveraging its relationship with the US ties has produced some results. Whenever Indo-US relations have been on a visibly higher trajectory, China has displayed a certain anxiety. Whether Wen Jiabao's wish to visit New Delhi soon after Obama's a manifestation of this anxiety, is a question worth pondering.

Obama's visit itself has had a very positive impact on Indo-US relations. He was able to address many irritants like the banned entity list, export of dual-use technology and support for a permanent seat in the UNSC and came out with formulations favourable to India. This shows a certain upgradation in the quality of the bilateral relations. This will, no doubt, be watched very carefully by China. Obama's remark in Parliament on the need for India to not only 'look east' but also 'engage east' is very relevant. So is the reference in the Joint Statement to 'a open, balanced and inclusive architecture in Asia'.

While the areas of commonalities between India and US are many, sheer real-politik, the economic muscle of China and the weakening of US power would compel America to be cautious in its dealings with China. India's strategy should be to increase its indispensability to both China and the US.

References

Bergsten, Fred, Bates Gill, Nicholas Lardy and Derek Mitchell (2006). *China: The Balance Sheet*. Centre for Strategic and International Studies and the Institute for International Economics.

Clegg, Jenny (2009). *China's Global Strategy: Towards a Multipolar World.*

Economic and Political Weekly (2010). *China after 1978: Craters on the Moon*. Orient Blackswan.

Eisenman, Joshua (2007). "China's Post Cold War Strategy in Africa: Examining Beijing's Methods and Objectives", *China and the Developing World*: 29-59.

Fabre, Guilhem (2010). "The Twilight of "Chimerica"? China and the Collapse of the American Model", *Working Paper No.* 06/WP/2009. Department of Economics, Ca Foscari University of Venice.

Fogel, Robert (2010). *Foreign Policy*, Jan/Feb 2010

Foot, Rosemary (2010). "China and the United States: Between Cold and Warm Peace", *Survival* 51(6), December-January.

Hachigian, Nina and Peng Yuan (2010). "The US-China Expectations Gap: An Exchange", *Survival* 52(4), August-September.

Hiro, Dilip (2010). *After Empire: The Birth of a Multipolar World.*

Jha, Prem Shankar (n.d.). *India and China: The Battle between Soft and Hard Power*.

Kennedy, Andrew B. (2010). "China's New Energy Security Debate", *Survival* 52(5), June-July.

Malone, David R. and Rohan Mukherjee (2010). "India and China: Conflict and Cooperation", *Survival* 52(1), February.

Mandelbaum, Michael (2006). *The Frugal Superpower: America's Global Leadership in a Cash-Strapped Era.*

Rudd, Kevin (2010). "A New Sinology", *Times of India,* May 4.

Saunders, Phillip C. (2009). "Managing Strategic Competition with China", *Strategic Forum* No.242, July.

Sutter, Robert (2010). *United States and China: Will Positive Relations Endure?* (*www.eastasiaforum.org 9/28/2010*)

Thompson, Drew (2010). "China's Military", *Foreign Policy,* March/April.

Yan, Xuetong (2010). "The Instability of China-US Relations", *The Chinese Journal of International Politics* 3: 263-292.

Zhang, Baohui (2010). "Chinese Foreign Policy in Transition: Trends and Implications", *Journal of current Chinese Affairs* 2.

8 China-EU Relations

H.H.S. Viswanathan

PRC-EU diplomatic relations are more than 35 years old. Established in 1975, the 30th anniversary was celebrated in 2005 with much fanfare. The relationship has made considerable progress in trade and investment; the EU is today China's largest trading partner and China is the second largest trading partner for EU after the US. European companies have been increasing their foreign direct investments into China in the last two decades and this has benefitted both sides. At the same time, for various reasons, EU-PRC relations have not developed into a meaningful strategic partnership. What has been advised is that both China and EU realise that there are no fundamental conflicts of interests and that neither side poses a threat to the other. There is also a broad similarity in their approaches to international issues with both sides preferring multilateralism and non-military solutions.

In 2003, EU and China established a 'Comprehensive Strategic Partnership' however, this did not qualitatively change the nature of their engagement. The existence of a Strategic Partnership does not necessarily mean that there is an effective strategy. Both sides have taken efforts to correct this, but there are some fundamental institutional problems.

At the end of the Cold War, China had great hopes of working with the EU in creating a truly multipolar world. Nor being adequately strong economically and politically, and facing an international cold shoulder after the Tiananmen incidents of 1989, China was vulnerable and nowhere in a position to challenge the sole superpower, US. Creation of a multi-polar world together was a viable option for both China and Europe. The Chinese formulation for the international situation at that time was that 'the old order has ended and the new one is yet to take shape'. China hoped to work with EU in realising the new order, but it was disappointed by the ineffectiveness of Europe in the task. What China saw was an inward looking EU, busy with expansion of the organisation. Here, China saw a contradiction: while the EU believed that a larger organisation would add strength to it, what actually happened was a disparate Union with countries at different economic levels leading to the weakening of the Union. Another contradiction was the intense desire of the new entrants from the erstwhile Warsaw Pact region to protect their newly obtained sovereignty without any dilution, which made EU's decision-making all the more complicated. The US role in the eastward expansion of NATO and in the former Yugoslavia, which was EU's own backyard was seen by China as an indication of EU's weakness in dealing with US.

One factor that seriously affects China-EU relations today, as indeed in the past, is the US angle which has primacy in their respective foreign policies. This factor has been both the cause and the effect of a weak China-EU relationship. There was an opportunity to correct this in 2003, after the US military operation in Iraq. Statements made by both sides during that period reflected implied concerns of US 'unilateralism' and the need for a more 'multipolar' world. Between 2003 and 2006, there was hectic diplomatic activity by both China and individual EU members countries, as well as EU Commissioners. However, these led only to the strengthening of bilateral relations with individual countries, while the relationship with the EU as a whole remained static.

China's turnover of trade in goods with the EU in 2009 was 297 billion Euros (215 billion Euros in exports and 82 billion Euros in imports). The same year, the EU exported 18 billion Euros worth of services and, the value of services imported was 13 billion Euros. EU's investment in China in 2009 was 5.3 billion Euros while in the reverse direction, it amounted to 0.3 billion Euros. Apart from trade, there have been other areas of significant cooperation—S&T, maritime transport, tourism, customs cooperation and nuclear energy. The project GALILEO, the civil global navigation satellite system and the multilateral agreement on the International Thermonuclear Experimental Reactor (ITER) project on nuclear fusion, are specially cited as excellent examples of cooperation in the S&T sector.

Challenges for China-EU Strategic Relations

The first challenge is the institutional constraint. EU may be the most integrated area in the world enjoying a single market and a common currency in 16 countries, but this does not make the EU a single player. Even after the Lisbon Treaty of 2009 and the appointment of a High Representative for Foreign Affairs and Security Policy, the EU is still inter-governmental in nature. This has resulted in China seeking out member countries for bilateral ties which had led to a rivalry among them for securing the best economic gains.

Human Rights Issues

EU is one of the most ardent advocates of Human Rights. It's founding treaty (Treaty on European Union 1993) established 'democracy and rule of law, and respect for human rights and fundamental freedoms' as the basic objective of EU's Common Foreign and Security Policy (CFSP). Over the years, the EU concern for human rights was played out ritually every year in the United Nations Human Rights Council (UNHRC), where EU would routinely sponsor a draft resolution critical of China's human rights record. Things came to a head in 1997 at the 53rd meeting of UNHRC. Even though the draft resolutions were largely symbolic and China would eventually block them by a maneuver called 'no action motion', China showed particular keenness to put an end to this yearly ritual. Using its economic leverage, it was able to lure the heavy weights—Germany, France, Spain and Italy away from such resolutions. The differences within the EU on this issue and China's threat to countries like Denmark which wanted to go ahead with the resolution had long-term consequences. A new *modus vivendi* was found by which, the 'common position' would take the form of a statement of the EU Presidency at the UNHRC. Thus, the Human Rights issue was made into a 'dialogue'. Though the high profile nature of the criticism in UNHRC has been done away with, EU continues to express its reservations on the issue, and asserts that its EU expectations 'are increasingly not being met'.

The difference over Human Rights reached its zenith after the Tiananmen events of June 1989. EU condemned, in no uncertain terms, the 'brutal repression by China'. It suspended all high-level contacts, postponed new projects and exerted considerable diplomatic pressure in multilateral fora. Most significantly, EU also imposed an 'arms embargo' on China that continues to be on place to the present day.

Arms Embargo

This is a major irritant which China would like to see removed early. To this end, it has been working on Germany and France which have been more amendable to lifting the ban. But there is strong resistance from the Scandinavian countries and Netherlands, all very strong advocates of human rights. The embargo itself is more symbolic in nature and is not very effective. There is no list of prohibited items and more importantly it is not a part of EU law and this has led to different interpretations. Some say there should be a freeze on all arms sales while others feel it applies only to lethal weapons. It is significant that even with the ban in place, arms sales licences approved for China have shown a steady growth.

Tibet

Tibet is a very serious issue which flares up from time to time. The EU has given high priority to early Chinese ratification of the International Covenant on Civil and Political Rights (ICCPR), on which China is not showing any keenness. Chancellor Angela Merkel's meeting with Dalai Lama in September 2007 and that of President Sarkozy in 2008 elicited very sharp criticism from China, and led to a dampening of economic relations. China had the EU-China Summit of 2008 postponed because of France holding the Presidency at that time.

Taiwan

This is a less contentious issue in China-EU relations if one compares it to China-US relations. EU's official policy has always followed the 'one China principle'. Nonetheless, China does not take the situation for granted and is ever vigilant because Taiwan is EU's third largest trading partner in Asia. A growing economic engagement could increase Taiwan's clout in the Union. EU has, at times, expressed concern over China's rejection of use of force to resolve the issue.

Competition between the Various EU Countries

This has been the most important factor in the weakening of a common EU position *vis-à-vis* China. Conversely, this has been the best opening for China to pursue its own interests. The economic and commercial advantages that China offers are too tempting for the individual countries—particularly the large ones like Germany, France and UK—to sacrifice for the sake of a common EU approach. The UNHRC and arms embargo are classic cases where individual economic gains have dictated the course of action taken by member states. In both cases, countries which are sympathetic to the Chinese point of view have succeeded in getting substantial benefits.

Trade-related Issues

Given the fact that the underpinning of relations is economic and commercial, trade-related issues attain great significance. The EU supported China's entry into the WTO in 2001. However, its reluctance to grant China market economy status has been seen by China as an unfriendly act. So far 97 countries throughout the world have granted China this status, but not the US, EU, Japan, India and a few others. It is vital for China to secure this status as a means to assume fairer treatment in anti-dumping probes. In any case, by 2016, China has to be given this status under the terms of China's accession to WTO in 2001; but China would like to have it earlier since most of the new anti-dumping cases are directed against China.

The EU's trade deficit with China is an issue which regularly hits the headlines in European mass media. The deficit has been increasing steadily, causing concern in European capitals and the EU headquarters in Brussels, particularly when EU economies are doing badly. One related issue on this is the European criticism of China keeping its currency, the RMB, at an artificially low level, thus making its products more competitive. Market access to European products into China is another area of dispute. The current 'indigeneous innovation drive' in China is seen in Europe as discriminatory and providing a non-level playing field for the European companies *vis-à-vis* the Chinese state owned enterprises. IPR and complaints of shoddy and dangerous products (such as toys and food items with toxic elements) have become regular topics of heated discussion in China-EU trade.

How trade dominates China-EU relations is highlighted by incidents like the so-called 'Bra Wars' (my apologies to the ladies), a term coined by the UK media on the dispute over a surge in the export of textile items from

China in 2005. The EU blocked consignments of 80 million items including pullovers, trousers, etc., soon after the introduction of free trade in these items after the formal ending of the Multi-Fibre Agreement (MFA). Under the 'anti-surge provision' for the first three years, EU took this measure due to pressure from European businesses. The dispute became unpleasant and prolonged. It was finally resolved in September 2005 during Prime Minister Blair's visit to Beijing. China agreed not to export anymore of these items during that year and further, to treat half of those already exported against the 2006 quota.

Climate Change

Climate Change is an issue where the EU has serious differences with China. While accepting historic responsibility for global warming in the past and having agreed to unilateral cuts in carbon emissions, EU feels that China, though a low level polluter in the past, must do much more now since, as of today, it is one of the highest polluters. The EU certainly did not like the way US cut a deal at the Copenhagen Summit in 2009 with the BASIC countries leaving the EU out in the cold.

China's Increasing Influence in Africa

Another area of concern for EU, particularly the ex-colonial powers like the UK, France, Spain and Portugal is the impressive penetration of China in Africa. Countries which were literally under the domination of ex-colonial masters in the post-independent, neocolonial period are now under the economic influence of China. In fact, many of them even admire the Chinese model of growth and development. The EU countries are themselves to blame for this state of affairs. After the end of the Cold War, Africa was totally neglected by Europe and left to fend for itself. The complementarities of the Chinese and African economies (China needs the natural resources and Africa needs investments) provided an ideal opportunity for China to move into Africa in a big way. There is also an indication that many African countries appreciate Chinese assistance because it is not accompanied by interference in their internal affairs. In their attempt to catch up with China, EU countries are adopting strategies which could well be alienating them further from Africa, like the recent

'Raw Materials Initiative' which seeks to retaliate against African countries putting restrictions on export of raw materials without value addition.

Bilateral Relations

Realising fully the limitations of expanding relations with EU as a whole, and the advantages that can be derived from the rivalry between the member states, China has assiduously cultivated bilateral relations, particularly with the bigger EU member countries notably Germany, France and the UK. In fact, 70 per cent of China's trade with the EU is with just five countries i.e., the above three along with the Netherlands and Italy.

Germany, is by far the most important trade partner for China. The bilateral trade of $115 billion is equal to China's trade with UK, France and Italy combined. That is why there was concern that Chancellor Merkel's meeting with the Dalai Lama in September 2007 could jeopardise the strong economic ties that the EU had established with China. Indeed there was a brief downturn, but gradually commercial interest prevailed, and normalcy in relations was restored. Germany is one of the few countries which have a favourable balance of trade with China and companies like Audi, BMW and Daimler-Benz are doing very well in China. The 2008 financial crisis cut trade volume by 12.5 per cent and it is expected that it will take a few years before the original levels are reached. Chancellor Merkel's visit to China in July 2010 to reinvigorate the relationship led to an agreement to develop a 'strategic partnership'.

Even though France recognised the PRC in 1964, it was only after the 'global strategic partnership' agreed on in 2001, that one saw a meaningful, and steady growth of bilateral relations in all fields—political, economic, commercial, scientific, technical and cultural. Many high-level visits have been exchanged over in the last decade. Franco-Chinese cooperation in the nuclear sector illustrates a long-term industrial partnership. For 20 years, AREVA, Alstom and EDF have played a key role in setting up nuclear power plants in Daya Bay and Ling Ao. Large French companies like Michelin, Veolia, Lafarge and of course, Airbus have huge stakes in China.

President Sarkozy's meeting with the Dalai Lama in Poland in 2008 caused a serious set back in the bilateral relations, and China, as expected, reacted angrily. There were also problems in the movement of the Olympic torch in Paris, as a reaction to the brutal suppression of protests in Tibet in the spring of 2008. However, there appears to have been a return to normalcy, particularly with the high profile visit of President Hu Jintao to France in November 2010. French companies signed contracts worth over $20 billion, a welcome development for the French economy reeling under a recession and massive unemployment. The major beneficiaries were Areva and Airbus. It is understood that China will be purchasing two more nuclear reactors $4 billion worth of uranium from Areva, and 36 aircraft from Airbus as well as Sarkozy made no reference to human rights or to the jailed Chinese dissident Liu Xiaobo, who was awarded the Nobel Peace Prize earlier in 2010.

As regards the UK, the major bilateral issue in the past was the question of Hong Kong. With the handing over of the territory in 1997 and the adoption by China of the principle of 'One country, two systems' this issue seems to have been resolved to mutual satisfaction. However, from time to time, there are complaints from liberal groups in Hong Kong about Chinese attempts to tighten controls.

The United Kingdom was the first major western country to recognise the PRC in 1950 and in 1954 established diplomatic relations at the Charge d' affairs level, to be upgraded to ambassadorial level in 1972.

The recent takeover by a Conservative coalition government has been seen by China as a favourable development. Traditionally, China has preferred Conservative governments in UK for three reasons—they advocate open markets and free trade; they are more independent of the EU, and their policies are less affected by trade union pressures to act against 'dumping' of Chinese products. They are also traditionally more pragmatic on human rights. On the other hand, they tend to follow more closely the US lead on major foreign policy issues and could be swayed by American concepts of 'containment' to traditional.

The recent visit to China by PM David Cameron, accepted by the biggest ever business delegation has been described as a great success in terms of business deals. Like, Sarkozy, Cameron also did not take up the question of Liu Xiaobo. However, referred to the need for political reforms to keep pace with economic progress at a lecture (at the Beijing University).

The constraints faced by the EU in working and an effective unified policy on global issues have been both a problem and blessing for China. On the one hand, this has been an impediment to forging a meaningful strategic partnership, on the other, this has blunted the impact of anti-China actions on human rights and Tibet. In sum, China finds it much easier to deal with the members individually.

Implications for India

The strength of India's relations with EU also rests on bilateral engagement with the member states because of the same institutional constraint that applies to EU's dealings with China. Though there is a regular strategic dialogue with the EU as a whole, the outcomes of these are more general in nature. Unlike China, India does not have any long standing irritant with EU countries. On the other hand, India's relations with countries like France, the UK and Germany are very broad and deep. After the nuclear tests in 1998, France was the only western country which showed the requisite degree of sensitivity for our position. Earlier, they had also supplied fuel for the Tarapore Atomic Power Station, when the US had reneged on their commitments. Trade with these two countries as well as FDIs from them have also been steadily growing. With Germany, we have a special relationship under the framework of G-4 for getting a seat in the UNSC as a permanent member. These factors have not escaped China's notice. Similarly, the visit of David Cameron to India recently when he made extremely favourable statements (particularly against Pakistani sponsored terrorism) is a development that China has to take into account.

India's competition with China *vis-à-vis* Europe will be on the commercial, economic and technological fields. Both will continue to fight for European markets and inflows of FDI and transfer of the latest technologies. Just as China leverages its trade ties with European countries for political advantages, India could use its good political relations to enhance economic and technological cooperation.

References

Barysch, K., C. Grant and M. Leonard (2005). *Embracing the Dragon: EU's Partnership with China.* Centre for European Reform.

Breslin, Shaun (2004). *Beyond Diplomacy? UK Relations with China since 1997.* Political Studies Association.

Clegg, Jenny (2009). *China's Global Strategy: Towards a Multipolar World.*

Eisenman, Joshua (2007). "China's Post Cold War Strategy in Africa: Examining Beijing's Methods and Objectives", *China and the Developing World* 29-59.

Fogel, Robert (2010). *Foreign Policy.* January/February 11-19.

Glen, Carol M. and Richard C. Murgo (2007). *EU China Relations: Balancing Political Challenges with Economic Opportunities*. Springer-Verlag online. June 14.

Hiro, Dilip (2010). After Empire: The Birth of a Multipolar World.

Holslag, Jonathan (2010). "The Strategic Dissonance between Europe and China", *The Chinese Journal of International Politics* 3: 325-345.

Jha, Prem Shankar (2010). *India and China: The Battle between Soft and Hard Power.*

Malik, V.P. and Jorg Schultz (eds.) (2008). *The Rise of China: Perspectives from Asia and Europe.*

Mlone, David R. and Rohan Mukherjee (2010). "India and China: Conflict and Cooperation", *Survival* 52(1), February.

Rudd, Kevin (2010). "A New Sinology", *Times of India,* May 4.

Saunders, Philipp C. (2009). "Manging Strategic Competition with China", *Strategic Forum* No.242, July.

Snyder, Francis (2010). *European Union and China, 1949-2008: Basic Documents and Commentary.*

Xiang, Lanxin (2009). "Chinese Outlook on European Security", in T. Tardy (ed.), *European Security in a Global Context: Internal and External Dynamics*. Routledge.

Xie, Dehao (2010). "Where will China- Britain Relations go?", *China Daily,* 14 May.

Zhang, Baohui (2010). "Chinese Foreign Policy in Transition: Trends and Implications", *Journal of Current Chinese Affairs* 2.

Zhengde, H (2005). "Sino-EU Strategic Relationship", *Journal of International Studies* 2(1): 104-121.

9 Russia-China Relations

Uneasy Friendship?

Nandan Unnikrishnan and Ajish P. Joy

Over the past couple of decades, China and Russia have managed to forge one of the most enigmatic partnerships of the 21st century. Slowly and steadily, they have sorted out most of the irritants that hampered their bilateral ties. Border disputes have been settled amicably. There is much engagement and cooperation on multiple fronts. Overall economic relations and energy cooperation are growing. On nearly all major geopolitical issues, there is some understanding and not many serious divergences. There is an impressive record of high-level exchanges in 2010 alone. There were six meetings between Chinese President Hu Jintao and Russian President (2008-2012) Dmitry Medvedev. Medvedev has commented that the 'relations between Russia and China are at their highest point now.'[1] In public statements, the top leaderships of Russia and China appear to be in sync with each other about the direction in which the world should evolve. The stress on the multipolar system, the pre-eminent stature of the United Nations, opposition to the use of force and non-interference in the internal affairs of other countries figure prominently in the joint communiqués issued routinely by the two countries. Russia and China also 'stress traditional interpretations of national sovereignty rather than the promotion of universal democratic values or other ideologies.'[2] Therefore, it would appear that Sino-Russian relations have not only been better than ever but likely to strengthen further. However, as Andrew Kuchins (2009) suggests, 'the history of China-Russia relations does not set the highest of bars.'

This paper argues that the possibilities of divergence between Russia and China are real, and as a result, the present Sino-Russian bonhomie

---

1. *People's Daily Online* (2010).
2. Weitz (2008).

may face serious challenges. As the disparity between their national power increases, it is likely that both countries will revisit their relationship. Russia presently is facing the dilemma of being relegated into the status of a junior partner and unless it finds a way to broad-base its economy, it will have to live in the ignominy of being a resource appendage to China (and Europe). In such a scenario, tensions cannot be ruled out between the two neighbours and the Far East and Central Asia may prove to be battlegrounds where the rivalry will play out. This is likely to affect trade ties, including the energy partnership, because the two countries have divergent concepts of energy security. Moreover, their respective strategic outlooks have some contradictions which make the possibility of divergence real.

When great powers and emerging powers also happen to be neighbours, rarely do they share cordial relations. Modern European history bears testimony to this fact. The 20th century superpowers had docile neighbours (the United States had Canada and Mexico while the Soviet Union had its satellites; China was an exception). With China, which was its only belligerent neighbour, the Soviet Union had a military confrontation. Similarly, as Russia tries to regain its stature in the international system and China continues its relentless growth, their strategic partnership may prove to be tenuous.

Ambiguous Strategic Partnership

Russia and China today qualify their relationship as a truly strategic one. However, while they may share the vision on how the world should evolve, the present closeness between the two is driven by tactical pragmatism rather than convergence of long-term strategic interests. For example, in spite of all talks about Eurasianism and Asian affinity, Russia at heart remains a Western power and its orientation is and will remain towards Europe and the West. The Chinese with their 'Middle-Kingdom' perception differs on this account. As Bobo Lo (2006) argues,

> It is not for nothing that [Prime Minister] Putin insists that Russia is an integral part of European civilisation or that he reiterates his commitment to democracy, the rule of law, and civil society. This is not just a crude attempt to curry favour with the West, but reflects a deeper conviction that modern Russian norms and values more closely approximate those of the West than the East. Whatever their differences, Russia sees itself as existentially intertwined with the West. Conversely, irrespective of how much they may agree, Russia continues to view China as essentially foreign.

Both China and Russia see ties with the US as their primary strategic relationship and in pursuance of a healthy relationship with the US, they could demote the significance of their bilateral ties. Already, Russia is bothered about its diminishing status on the global scene. The talks of a US-China condominium—a G-2—was quite unsettling for Russia and the acute fear of being relegated to a peripheral status forces Russia to play the 'China card' against the West.

Another area of possible Sino-Russian divergence is Russia's keen awareness of its limitations as far as its technological requirements are concerned. Russia knows full well that the cutting-edge technology which is required to drag it out of the morass caused by the global financial crisis can come only from the West, not China. In this regard, the Russians already have a role model in Tsar Peter the Great who in an attempt to modernise Russia travelled to Europe under a pseudonym, to study 'European advances in shipbuilding, fire-fighting, dentistry, lock-smithing and parliamentary procedure, among other cutting-edge technologies.'[3]

Possible Russian thinking in this regard was revealed in a leaked Russian foreign ministry document which appeared in the Russian *Newsweek* magazine in May 2010. The document stresses the need for Russia to pursue 'modernization alliances—especially with the United States and major EU states such as Germany, France, and Italy—in which Russia offers investment opportunities and greater political cooperation in exchange for foreign capital and know-how.'[4] The document noted that Western technology and investment is crucial to Russia's development. Interestingly, the document also contained a rare official swipe at China to the effect that Russia needs to 'proceed from the assumption that we need to hold China to acting in concert with Russia in international forums, where they need our help more than we need theirs.'[5] Russia is also confident about the fact that its interests in regions adjoining the West like Georgia and Ukraine are now safer than ever; forcing the West to limit its ambitions like the eastward expansion of NATO.

3. Barry (2010).
4. Mankoff (2010).
5. Weir (2010).

Russia and China in Central Asia

As China continues to grow at a rapid pace, there are two important geographic regions—Central Asia and the Far East—where Sino-Russian tensions can be a real possibility. Central Asia is likely to be one of the key geographical theatres in which Sino-Russian friendship will be tested. Russia considers Central Asia as its near abroad (*blizhneye zarubezhye*) and believes that it should remain under Russia's 'liberal imperialism.'[6] Russia's overall strategy in Central Asia is to maintain its influence in the region, keep the Central Asian Republics politically stable, ensure that the Russia-leaning elites stay in power, check the spread of Islamic extremism and finally, to ensure that the Russian stranglehold over the energy outflow from the region remains in place. Russia's concerns and interests in Central Asia were officially reaffirmed in its Foreign Policy Concept and the New Defence Law published in 2008. These documents speak about Russia's privileged interests in the post-Soviet space, and do not rule out the possibility of military intervention in case of threats to Russian minority interests and national dignity or if there is aggression against Russian forces stationed in these territories.[7]

China shares with Russia several strategic objectives regarding Central Asia. Political stability, suppression of terrorism and uninterrupted supply of energy are important concerns for China. The unease about sustained American presence in their backyard is another concern that China and Russia share in Central Asia. Russia has been cooperating with China in Central Asia primarily because of these shared interests so long as the status quo is maintained—in which China cedes to Russia the predominant role in Central Asia. However, this situation may not last for long.

The global financial crisis could be a turning point in this context as the Russian economy contracted by about 8 per cent in 2008 while the Chinese economy grew by the same percentage. Since Moscow was hit hard by the crisis, it was forced to scale back many of its projects in Central Asia and renegotiate the terms of unprofitable regional energy deals.[8]

6. Aslund (2010).
7. "The New Foreign Policy Concept of the Russian Federation President of Russia". July 12, 2008, *http://archive.kremlin.ru/eng/text/docs/2008/07/204750.shtml*
8. Cooley (2009).

As a result, China got an opening in Central Asia to assert its presence and it utilised the opportunity by investing massively in the region. In 2009–10, for the first time in history, China's net trade with the Central Asian region exceeded that of Russia.[9] China also managed to lay energy pipelines from Central Asia bypassing Russia—something that has never happened before. The Turkmenistan-China pipeline—part of the Central Asia-China Gas Pipeline—with a maximum discharge capacity of 40bcm/year was inaugurated in December 2009. China invested nearly $3 billion for setting up the pipeline. In Kazakhstan, the China National Petroleum Corporation (CNPC) along with KazMunayGas operates the recently opened 2200 km long oil pipeline linking Atyrau to Xinjiang. China already has an 11 per cent stake in KazMunaiGas (KMG). MangistauMunaiGas (MMG), a major oil producer has been taken over by the CNPC for $2.6 billion. China Development Bank has offered the Kazakh copper company Kazakhmys a $2.7 billion loan to develop the Boschekul mines with an annual capacity of 100,000 tonnes of copper cathode.

China is also gradually developing Central Asia into a transport hub which will help link it to Europe through Kyrgyzstan and Uzbekistan. In Tajikistan, China plans to invest more than a billion dollars to set up road networks, power plants and power grids. These projects may eventually lead to the integration of the Central Asian economy into that of China. This development may help the Chinese in increasing their political influence as well. Russia is deeply suspicious about these transport networks and it favours the North-South Transport corridor linking Russia, Iran, India and Central Asia and keeping China out. In fact, there are scholars who argue that Russia perceives China's development of the port at Gwadar in Pakistan as conflicting with its own goals.[10]

China also engages with the Central Asian countries, especially Kyrgyzstan and Kazakhstan, through border trade. China is a member of Central Asia Regional Economic Cooperation (CAREC) in which all Central Asian states except Turkmenistan are members. China has set up a number of free trade zones close to border crossings with Kazakhstan and Kyrgyzstan. Meanwhile these countries have opened consulates in

9. Indeo (2010).

10. Carlson (2007).

Urumqi to cater to the Chinese businessmen. Such enhanced cooperation has led to Chinese migration and settlements in Central Asian states. In December 2009, China had revealed a plan to lease a million hectares of land in Kazakhstan for farming. This scheme, if successfully implemented, will further entrench Chinese presence in Central Asia. With its economic might and demographic muscle, China is outpacing Russia in Central Asia. The situation has been pithily described by a Central Asian observer: 'China doesn't only buy loyalty with documents, but with money given at a low percentage.'[11]

Even the Shanghai Cooperation Organisation (SCO) which was hailed as the new template for Sino-Russian cooperation in Central Asia has witnessed instances of strategic divergences and manifestations of the economic disparity between Russia and China. Russia is uncomfortable with the China's increasing influence in SCO. The failure to get the SCO endorsement at the Dushanbe Summit (2008) for its military action against Georgia and the independence of Abkhazia and South Ossetia was a blow to Moscow.[12] Meanwhile, China was successful in winning SCO support during the outbreak of violence between the Uighur Muslims and Han Chinese in Urumqi, in July 2009.[13] As the world was grappling with the financial crisis, China set up a $10 billion stabilisation fund for the SCO countries in order to provide soft loans for the member countries. Russia was unable to co-finance the fund as it was reeling from the crisis and a contracting economy. The Chinese attempt to create a free trade zone among the SCO countries has alarmed not only Russia, but also the Central Asian states. Russia counters this plan with a possible expansion of the Eurasian Economic Community (EurAsEC) which includes Russia, Kazakhstan, Kyrgyzstan, Tajikistan and Belarus, keeping China out. The creation of a customs union between Belarus, Kazakhstan and Russia was another attempt at closing ranks on the trade front. On the military/strategic front in Central Asia, Russia prefers the Collective Security Treaty Organization (CSTO) in which Russia, Armenia, Belarus, Kazakhstan, Kyrgyzstan and Tajikistan are members.

11. The Economist (2010).

12. Katz (2008).

13. Cooley (2009).

The Russian Far East

Another potential theatre for Sino-Russian rivalry is the Russian Far East with which China shares a long border. The Far East (Dalny Vostok Rossii) is a vast swathe of territory that lies between Lake Baikal and Vladivostok with an area of 6 million sq km, but with just about 6.5 million inhabitants. On the other side of the border, just across the Amur River, lie the three Manchurian provinces of China-Heilongjiang, Jilin and Liaoning—with around 110 million people between them. While the Chinese population grows at a sustained pace, the Russian Far East is steadily losing people. 'This vast disparity between the neighbours, unmatched anywhere else in the world, can only grow in the years ahead. This would probably create tension even without another crucial factor.'[14] As S.C.M. Paine (1996) argues, 'if Russia and China were ever to engage each other militarily in the future it would be over control of the border regions.' Moreover, the Russian Far East is rich in natural resources and contains nearly all of Russia's diamonds, 70 per cent of its gold and substantial deposits of oil, natural gas, coal, timber, silver, platinum, tin, lead and zinc, as well as rich fishing grounds.[15]

Years of neglect, financial constraints and flawed policies have led to the economic stagnation of the Far East. The problem got accentuated with the disintegration of the Soviet Union. Under Soviet rule, the Far East economy was propped up by credits and money transfers. The region was also home to industrial plants specialising in defence and resource extraction. The Far East economy was 'closely tied to the rest of the Soviet Union and was shielded from the external world in order to maximize its utilization to Moscow's benefit.'[16] After the Soviet Union unravelled, the military presence in the region dwindled, factories were shut and people moved out in droves. Chronic corruption and mismanagement by the local authorities further aggravated the situation. While the Russian Far East was declining rapidly, across the border, China was scripting one of the most riveting economic turnarounds in history. The gross mismatch between the two adjacent regions has forced the Russian President to acknowledge

14. Blair (2009).
15. Kucera (2010).
16. Chang (1999).

that 'unless China invested in large-scale projects in the Far East, Moscow's plans to develop the region would not materialize.'[17] He added that the development strategy of the region must be 'coordinated in tandem with China's regional strategy of rejuvenating its old industrial base in Northeast China.'

While Russia welcomes Chinese investments in the region and supports coordinated development, there is an underlying tension. Although Russia and China have satisfactorily concluded their border treaties, there are lingering doubts about the Far East, especially because of the nature of Russian expansion in the region in the 19th century. The Treaties of Aigun (1858) and Peking (1860) which gave the Russian empire control over most of the Far East were concluded on unfavourable terms to the Chinese (Qing dynasty). This historical fact along with the mismatched demographics and China's steady growth has created some insecurity among the Russians regarding the future of the Far East. While the stories about the 'demographic assault' by China by means of aggressive migration into the Russian Far East are unsubstantiated to some extent, with China's rapid modernisation and growth, there will be an increased flow of Chinese migrants into Russia. Chinese investments will most likely bring Chinese contractors, managers and workers, a scenario which will not be to Moscow's liking.

There are several Russian commentators who posit that the future of the Russian Far East could be on the table in the next 15–20 years and the only way of guaranteeing Russia's territorial integrity is 'to trust in capabilities, not intentions.'[18] In September 2009, Russia's Chief of the Ground Forces Staff Lt. General Sergey Skokov observed that, 'in the east, Russia could face a multi-million-man army with a traditional approach to conducting combat operations: straightforward, with large concentrations of personnel and firepower along individual operational directions.' Commenting on this statement, leading Russian military expert Alexander Khramchikhin noted that 'for the first time since the early days of Gorbachev, a high-ranking national commander has de facto acknowledged officially that the People's Republic of China is the potential enemy.'[19] Interestingly, the Russian military exercise Vostok 2010 (in which over 20,000 troops,

17. Blank (2009).

18. Lo (2008).

19. Saradzhyan (2010).

75 combat aircrafts, 40 warships from the Pacific, Northern and Black Sea Fleets, and 5,500 pieces of heavy weapons took part) was held in the Far East. According to the Chief of the General Staff, General Nikolai Makarov, the exercise was aimed to 'maintain the security and defence of the state's national interests along its Far Eastern borders from a hypothetical enemy' (*uslovnyi protivnik*).[20] Bobo Lo rightly argues that while a Sino-Russian crisis is neither imminent nor inevitable, if Russia does not seriously wake up to the developmental challenges of the region, then notional risks could turn into realities, turning the Far East into a flash point.[21]

The Energy Conundrum

Prima facie, China-Russia trade relations is a match made in heaven. China will drive the global energy demand in the years to come, and by 2030 it is expected to consume about 16.3 m/d of oil. Meanwhile, its natural gas demand is set to reach about 651 bcm by 2030 according to International Energy Agency (IEA) estimates. Russia meanwhile has over 48 trillion cubic metres of discovered natural gas reserves, ranking first in the world and 200 billion tonnes of coal reserves, ranking second, apart from 6.5 billion tonnes of petroleum reserves. Russia and China share a very long land border with not many natural barriers separating them. China is keen to make use of these advantages as its appetite for hydrocarbons grows with its increased pace of modernisation and also because China wants to diversify its energy sources.

At present, nearly 45 per cent of the Chinese energy imports are from the Persian Gulf and the transport of energy from the region to China through the sea has been a security nightmare for China for quite some time. The Chinese are particularly concerned about the 'Malacca Dilemma' as they believe that whoever controls the Malacca Straits will control the energy flow to China as almost 90 per cent of China-bound oil passes through the straits. Terrorist attacks, piracy or intervention by the American, Japanese or the Indian navy can block the Malacca Straits, thereby seriously harming Chinese interests.[22] Therefore, China is trying

20. Kipp (2010).
21. *op cit.* no.18
22. Collins (2008).

to find as many overland alternatives as possible. Russia and Central Asia figure prominently in this regard. For example in February 2009, while the world was in the throes of the financial crisis, the China National Petroleum Corporation (CNPC) and the China Development Bank offered a loan of $25 billion to be shared between the Russian oil company Rosneft and the pipeline major Transneft. The loan was provided at a low interest rate of 5.7 per cent and in return China has been assured of annual oil supplies of 15 million tonnes for 20 years.

While the potential for extensive cooperation exists in the energy sector, the challenges are manifold. One big drawback is Russia's inherent reluctance to rely on the Chinese market and its focus on Europe. Even as the importance of China is on the rise, nearly all of Russia's natural gas exports and close to 80 per cent of its oil pipelines flow towards the West. Two factors, pricing and the fear of dependence on China, explain Russia's reluctance to become a key supplier to China. Russia and China are extremely price sensitive and in spite of the framework agreement signed between Gazprom and CNPC in 2009 for selling natural gas, further progress is held up by the issue of pricing. Russia has a lucrative deal with Europe in which gas prices are linked to the crude oil prices and China refuses to cut a deal on similar terms.

However, even as Russia increases its energy trade with China, it is difficult to believe that these countries will have a stable and confident energy partnership. For example, as a supplier, Russia is keen on demand security and as a consumer, China looks for supply security. As a result, both countries will always look for alternatives—Russia looks for diverse markets while China scouts for multiple sources. The Russian strategic planners will never be comfortable with China being Russia's principal market and will look to 'expand Russia's influence in other Asian energy markets such as Japan and South Korea while simultaneously reassuring Europe that it will continue to be Russia's biggest clients (East-West manoeuvring). China, for its part, fears it will be over-exposed to supply interruptions or reductions from Russia.'[23] A further clash of interests between Beijing and Moscow is possible as China gets increasingly active in the Central Asian energy scene which undercuts Russia's traditional advantage in the region. Bobo Lo

23. Mascotto (2010).

points out another interesting feature of the Russia-China energy relations: Russia wants to sell more natural gas to China, while China is keen on oil imports from Russia. The role of gas in China's energy mix is not very high, with projected figures of just around 8 per cent in 2020. This difference in priorities also affects the development of the energy trade between the two countries.

Another issue to be considered is the increasing Russian anxiety of ending up as a raw materials appendage of China. Indeed the nature of Russia-China trade looks increasingly so. Russia exports raw materials—not only oil, but timber, minerals, electricity, etc., to China, while China sends to Russia manufacturing goods, consumer electronics and durables, apparels, heavy machinery and automobiles. Although Russia also exports military hardware and jet engines to China, the scope of trade is considerably limited compared to the Soviet era. There is a growing fear in Russia that it is literally 'fuelling' Chinese growth, which in the long term will be detrimental to Russian interests.

To conclude, it is safe to argue that while Sino-Russian relations at present are infinitely better than any time in the past, there is no guarantee that it will remain so in the future. Pragmatism is the biggest driving force behind the bonhomie than any shared vision or values. Therefore, the possibility of rifts developing between these two continent-sized neighbours is real and there are several potential irritants that can lead to this scenario. As Russia grapples with possible relegation as a junior partner in this bilateral tandem, the present equation between China and Russia can easily change. The demographic imbalance, accentuated by geographic proximity, could create serious problems in the near future. Managing the respective interests of the two countries in Central Asia and the Far East is not going to be any easier. While economic ties have the potential to bind the two countries together, the nature of trade is not to Russia's advantage. In any case, both countries are not each other's biggest trading partners. With such potential roadblocks, it will be interesting to see how Russia and China carry forward their relations in an increasingly globalised world.

References

Aslund, Anders (2010). "The Kremlin's New Policy in Its Near Abroad", *The Moscow Times*, July 28, Available on *http://www.themoscowtimes.com/opinion/article/the-kremlins-new-policy-in-its-near-abroad/411170.html*

Barry, Ellen (2010). "In Czar Peter's Footsteps", *The New York Times*, May 29, Available on *http://www.nytimes.com/2010/05/30/weekinreview/30BARRY.html*

Blair, David (2009). "Why the Restless Chinese are Warming to Russia's Frozen East?", *The Telegraph*, July 16, Available on *http://www.telegraph.co.uk/comment/5845646/Why-the-restless-Chinese-are-warming-to-Russias-frozen-east.html*

Blank, Stephen (2009). "China Quietly Reshapes Asia", *Asiatimes Online*, August 12, Available on *http://www.atimes.com/atimes/China_Business/KH12Cb01.html*

Carlson, Brian (2007). "The Limits of Sino-Russian Strategic Partnership in Central Asia", *Journal of Public and International Affairs* 18: 174, Spring.

Chang, Felix K. (1999). "The Russian Far East's Endless Winter", *Orbis*, Spring. Available on *http://www.fpri.org/orbis/4301/chang.russiafareast.pdf*

Collins, Gabriel (2008). "An Oil Armada? The Commercial and Strategic Significance of China's Growing Tanker Fleet", in Toshi Yoshihara and James R Holer (eds.), *Asia Look Seaward: Power and Maritime Strategy*, Praeger, Westport. pp.111-124.

Cooley, Alexander (2009). "Cooperation Gets Shanghaied", *Foreign Affairs*, December 14. Available on *http://www.foreignaffairs.com/articles/65724/alexander-cooley/cooperation-gets-shanghaied?page=show*

Indeo, Fabio (2010). "Russia and China in Central Asia: Growing Geopolitical Competition", *ISPI Policy Brief* No. 199, October. Available on *http://www.ispionline.it/it/documents/PB_199_INDEO_2010.pdf*

Katz, Mark N. (2008). "Russia and the Shanghai Cooperation Organization: Moscow's Lonely Road from Bishkek to Dushanbe", *Asian Perspective* 32(3): 183-87. Available on *http://digilib.gmu.edu:8080/bitstream/1920/3340/1/russia_and_the_shanghai.pdf*

Kipp, Jacob W. (2010). "Vostok 2010 and the Very Curious Hypothetical Opponent", *Eurasia Daily Monitor* 7(133), July 12.

Kucera, Joshua (2010). "China's Russian Invasion", *The Diplomat*, February 19. Available on *http://the-diplomat.com/2010/02/19/china%E2%80%99s-russian-invasion/*

Kuchins, Andrew C. (2009). "Sino-Russian Myths", *Survival* 51(5): 185-92, October–November.

Lo, Bobo (2008). *Axis of Convenience: Moscow, Beijing, and the New Geopolitics*. Brookings Institution Press and Chatham House. p.71.

———. (2006). "China and Russia, Common Interests, Contrasting Perceptions", *CLSA Special Report*, May, p.13.

Mankoff, Jeffrey (2010). "Changing Course in Moscow", *Foreign Affairs*, September 7. Available on *http://www.foreignaffairs.com/articles/66743/jeffrey-mankoff/changing-course-in-moscow*

Mascotto, Guillaume (2010). "Demystifying Russia's Energy Strategy toward China: Strategic Manipulation or Unwitting Vulnerability?", *Cahier De Recherche – CEIM*, April. Available on *http://www.ieim.uqam.ca/IMG/pdf/MascottoG_Russia2010.pdf*

Paine, C.M.S. (1996). *Imperial Rivals: China, Russia, and their Disputed Frontier*. New York: ME Sharpe. p.355.

People's Daily Online (2010). "Medvedev: Sino-Russian Ties at Highest Point", *People's Daily Online*, September 28. Available on *http://english.peopledaily.com.cn/90001/90776/90883/7153214.html*

Saradzhyan, Simon (2010). "The Role of China in Russia's Military Thinking", *International Relations and Security Network*, May 4. Available on *http://belfercenter.ksg.harvard.edu/publication/20129/role_of_china_in_russias_military_thinking.html*

The Economist (2010). "China in Central Asia: Riches in the Near Abroad", *The Economist*, January 28. Available on *http://www.economist.com/node/15393705*

Weir, Freid (2010). "Leaked Russian document: Could Medvedev era tilt more pro-West?", *The Christian Science Monitor*, May 13. Available on *http://www.csmonitor.com/World/Europe/2010/0513/Leaked-Russian-document-Could-Medvedev-era-tilt-more-pro-West*

Weitz, Richard (2008). *China-Russia Security Relations: Strategic Parallelism without Partnership or Passion?*. Strategic Studies Institute, August, *http://www.strategicstudiesinstitute.army.mil/pdffiles/pub868.pdf*

10 China's Growing Role in Central Asia

Angira Sen Sarma

China over the years has gradually strengthened its position in the Central Asian region and has established strong bilateral ties with each of the five Central Asian Republics (CARs). China's major success has been its economic diplomacy, which has helped it to increase its influence in the region. China's primary interest in the region is gaining access to the rich energy resources. Three of the five CARs (Kazakhstan, Turkmenistan and Uzbekistan) are rich in hydrocarbon reserves. The other main Chinese interest in the region is to prevent the Uyghur cause from gaining support from the CARs. The Chinese policy towards Central Asia with regard to both these issues has been so far successful.

Since independence of these republics, the government to government relationship between the CARs and China have improved significantly. Three of the five CARs share border with China. The Sino-CARs border disputes, which were part of the Sino-Soviet border disputes, have been amicably resolved. Border Commissions with Russia, Kazakhstan and Kyrgyzstan have been established jointly to deal with border issues. The Shanghai Cooperation Organisation (SCO), a Chinese initiative, which was initially established as 'Shanghai 5' played an important role in resolving these border disputes. The 1996 SCO summit meeting began the process of demilitarisation and demarcation of borders between China and the CARs. Resolving this historical border disputes helped China and CARs to gradually improve their relations in other areas as well.

The CARs too have their own interest in developing closer ties with China. All five countries benefitted economically by moving close to China. It helped them to reduce their dependence on Russia, a dominant player in the region. Like Russia, China has never raised issues like democracy and human rights in its bilateral negotiations with these republics. These issues have been a major irritant in CARs relation with the West. China's silence on these issues has made the Central Asian governments comfortable working with it.

The paper argues that China today has emerged as a major economic partner for the CARs and it will remain an influential player in the region. The Central Asian region is also geo-politically and geo-strategically important for China, particularly as it borders the Xinjiang province of China. Economic development of the Xinjiang province, which is part of Chinese programme for quelling unrest in the region, has made the CARs strategically significant for China. Chinese interest in the region revolves around three-core interests 'security, development and energy'.[1] Because of its rich natural resources and geo-strategic location, Central Asia will in the future emerge as an area of competition between the various external players engaged in the region. China will be one of the main contenders in this contest.

China as a Major Economic Player

One of the prime driving forces behind Chinese interest in the region is the region's rich natural resources. China needs a secure and reliable supply of oil and gas to sustain its high economic growth. China is the second largest energy consumer in the world, and as its domestic production is unable to meet its growing demand, China has been looking for diverse sources of supply across the world. The bulk of China's hydrocarbon imports come from West Asia, which rely on sea routes for transportation. The CARs with rich reserves provide China with an alternative source of energy. China has made huge investments in constructing energy infrastructures in the region, which has helped China to gain foothold in the energy sector, which continue to be largely dominated by Russia. The completion of the Kazakhstan-China oil pipeline and the Turkmenistan-China gas pipeline are two major developments in the growth of Chinese engagement in the region.

The first section of the Kazakhstan-China oil pipeline connecting oilfields located in the Aktobe region with Atyrau (western Kazakhstan)

1. Clarke (2010).

was completed in 2003.[2] The second phase of the pipeline included the construction of the Atasu-Alashankou pipeline. The construction of the second segment of the Kazakhstan-China pipeline started in late September 2004, was completed in December 2005, and began operating in July 2006. The pipeline initially carried oil from the Kumkol field in central Kazakhstan; CNPC developed the field, which it acquired in 2005.[3] The final stage of the Kazakhstan-China pipeline was the Kenkiyak-Kumkol section, which is operating since July 2009.[4] The total length of the Kazakhstan-China pipeline is 1,860 miles.[5]

The 1,833-kilometre China-Central Asia gas pipeline originates from Gedaim at the Turkmenistan-Uzbekistan border crosses central Uzbekistan and southern Kazakhstan and finally reach Horgos in the northwest region of Xinjiang.[6] Two lines (each 1,833 km) of the pipeline will run parallel;[7] the first line became operational in December 2009. Back in 2007, CNPC signed a production sharing agreement with Turkmenistan to explore and develop gasfields on the right bank of the Amu Darya river and for Turkmenistan to supply 30 billion cubic metres of natural gas to China for a period of 30 years through the pipeline.[8] China also signed agreements with Kazakhstan and Uzbekistan for the gas pipeline. The mammoth task of building the pipeline traversing three countries (the first phase) was completed in less than 28 months.[9]

2. "Kazakhstan-China Pipeline" [Online: Web]. Accessed 8 October 2009, URL: *http://www.chinapage.com/transportation/pipeline/pipeline-kazakhstan.html*

3. "China-Kazakhstan Pipeline Starts to Pump Oil", 15 December 2005, [Online: Web] Accessed 12 November 2010, URL: *http://www.chinadaily.com.cn/english/doc/2005-12/15/content_503709.htm.*

4. "Kenkiyak-Kumkol Section of Kazakhstan-China oil pipeline becomes operational", 14 July 2009 [Online: Web] Accessed 12 October 2010, URL: *http://www.cnpc.com.cn/en/press/newsreleases/Kenkiyak_Kumkol_section_of_Kazakhstan%EF%BC%8DChina_Oil_Pipeline_becomes_operational.htm.*

5. *op. cit.* no. 2.

6. "Central Asia-China Gas Pipeline" [Online: Web]. Accessed 12 January 2011, URL: *http://www.cnpc.com.cn/en/aboutcnpc/ourbusinesses/naturalgaspipelines/Central_Asia%EF%BC%8DChina_Gas_Pipeline_2.htm.*

7. Ibid.

8. Ibid.

9. "Central Asia-China Gas Pipeline Operational", [Online: Web] Accessed 15 February 2011, URL: *http://www.cnpc.com.cn/en/press/Features/Flow_of_natural_gas_from_Central_Asia_.htm.*

Both these pipelines have far-reaching consequences for the region. They provide the landlocked CARs alternative routes to access international markets, which these republics have been looking for since their independence. Russia, which is the traditional player in the region's energy sector, controls all pipelines connecting the region with international markets. The CARs after independence have been trying to diversify their energy markets. Several pipelines bypassing Russia like Nabucco, Baku-Tbilisi-Ceyhan (BTC) Pipeline, TAPI etc., have been on the cards for many years. However, except for BTC none of these projects has made significant progress. China's major achievement has been the timely completion of these two pipelines, which has consolidated China's position as an important energy player in the region.

In addition to these two pipelines, China has invested in various other projects in the region's energy sector. China and Kazakhstan agreed for joint exploration and development of oil and gas resources in the Caspian Sea in 2004, CNPC paid US $4.2 billion to acquire PetroKazakhstan in 2005, China's International Trust and Investment Corporation got shares in oilfields in western Kazakhstan for US $1.9 billion.[10] AsiaTransGas, an Uzbekistan-China joint venture is yet another example of China's economic engagement in Central Asia.[11] In an agreement signed between the two countries, China got the right to refine oil and gas reserves in Uzbekistan and preferential access to wells after the drilling is completed.[12] China in 2009 gave US $4 billion to Turkmenistan to develop the South Yolotan gasfield, the largest gasfield in Turkmenistan.[13] In November 2009, CNPC and KazMunaiGas took over MangistauMuniGas, the Kazakh oil producer at a price of US $2.6 billion.[14] Kazakhstan in 2009 also received a loan of US $10 billion from China.[15] In 2009, China also agreed to invest US $1 billion

10. *op. cit.* no. 1.

11. Khodzhaev (2009).

12. Ibid.

13. The Economist, "Riches in the Near Abroad", 28 January 2010 [Online: Web]. Accessed on 14 October 2010, URL: *http://www.economist.com/node/15393705*

14. "FactBox-China in Central Asia: Latest Investments", 11 March 2010 [Online: Web]. Accessed 19 November 2010, URL: *http://www.reuters.com/assets/print?aid=USLDE6280UR20100311*

15. Ibid.

in Tajikistan to build power plants, electricity grids and roads in Tajikistan and in January 2010 China and Kyrgyzstan signed a deal to construct US $342 million electric grid link.[16]

Moreover, the large Central Asian market is an added attraction for China. Chinese finished products are abundantly available in the markets of Central Asia like Dordoi and Karasuu in Kyrgyzstan.[17] In Tajikistan too there are some Chinese and joint markets like Amindzhan, Shahrahe Abreshim, Bunyad-Shengong, Mostafa Artush, etc.[18] Also there are wholesale markets in Kazakhstan selling Chinese goods to other CARs and to regions in Russia bordering Central Asia.[19] Trade with the CARs got a boost with the creation of free economic zones (FEZ) in the border areas like in Chuguchak and Khorgos.[20]

In addition, China has invested in building roads in the region like the Irkeshtam-Osh road, the Osh-Uzgen road, some section of the Madaniyat-Shamaldyay-Tashkumyr-Razan road leading to the Krupsai hydroelectric station, etc.[21]

In recent years, China has emerged as one of the main trade partners of the CARs. Trade with China has significantly increased over the years. As the Table 10.1 shows, Kazakhstan is the main trade partner of China in the region ever since independence.

The tables hereafter set out the figures for the CARs's trade with the three major external players in the region—Russia, China and the US in the years 2008 and 2009.

16. Ibid.
17. Sadykzhan (2009).
18. Ibid.
19. Ibid.
20. Ibid: 50.
21. Ibid.

Table 10.1

China-Central Asia Trade

(Value: Million US$)

Countries	*1992*	*1993*	*1994*	*1995*	*1996*	*1997*	*1998*	*1999*	*2000*	*2001*	*2002*	*2003*	*2004*	*2005*	*2006*	*2007*	*2008*	*2009*
Kazakhstan	372.8	427.9	218.7	331.7	494.7	488.8	432.7	554.7	824.7	831.7	1336.0	2176.8	2725.5	6927.2	8506.0	14027.6	17825.4	14229.7
Kyrgyzstan	44.3	77.8	66.7	30.4	43.6	64.0	60.0	62.1	81.0	68.0	100.4	101.0	119.4	129.5	283.7	417.5	772.6	3224.1
Uzbekistan	54.8	57.5	131.3	116.5	177.6	194.9	93.1	41.9	54.3	62.7	139.5	343.0	554.20	663.2	961.1	1172.9	1705.5	1971.2
Tajikistan	2.8	10.6	6.2	6.0	7.5	15.3	5.8	5.2	15.3	7.4	9.7	32.4	63.1	98.2	158.8	283.6	466.5	816.5
Turkmenistan	4.5	4.2	4.0	7.7	11.4	7.0	6.1	13.5	16.4	59.8	109.7	104.9	93.9	99.5	178.7	332.5	883.3	1140.8

Source: Asian Development Bank (2010).

Table 10.2

Trade with Russia, China and the US (2008)

(Value: US Million Dollars)

Countries	*Russia*	*China*	*US*
Kazakhstan	20468	17825.4	2585.1
Kyrgyzstan	1802.4	772.6	119.8
Uzbekistan	3487.9	1705.5	330.6
Tajikistan	1171.8	466.5	-
Turkmenistan	891.3	883.3	200.9

Source: Asian Development Bank (2010).

Table 10.3

Trade with Russia, China and the US (2009)

(Value: US Million Dollars)

Countries	*Russia*	*China*	*US*
Kazakhstan	11514.2	14229.7	2112.3
Kyrgyzstan	1419.1	3224.2	57.1
Uzbekistan	2661.1	1971.2	107.1
Tajikistan	827.3	816.5	-
Turkmenistan	1033.8	1140.8	428.8

Source: Asian Development Bank (2010).

Chinese Security Interest in Central Asia

Security in the region is obvious of crucial interest to China. The Xinjiang region of China witnessing the Uyghur separatist movement shares border with three of the CARs. The Uyghurs, the majority population of the Xinjiang practice Islam and share Turkic culture, making them religiously and culturally closer to the CARs. There are about 250,000 Uyghurs in Kazakhstan, 50,000 in Kyrgyzstan and 40,000 in Uzbekistan.[22] Among the several ethnic groups found in Xinjiang, the region is also home to ethnic Kazakhs, Uzbeks and Kyrgyz. Through its diplomatic efforts, China has been successful in preventing the CARs from supporting the Uyghur separatist movement.

22. Dolkun (2007).

The governments of the CARs have repeatedly declared that they will not allow their territory to be used for the Uyghur movement and have crushed all groups supporting the cause. For example, Uzbekistan has strictly controlled any movement supporting the Uyghur cause in its territory—'fearing that Uzbekistan's Uighur movements, which support the Uighurs' struggle against the Chinese government, would negatively affect Sino-Uzbek relations, the Uzbek government has clamped down on the Uighur movements since independence.'[23] Since 1994, after Chinese Premier Li Peng's visit, Uzbekistan has repressed any Uyghur movement in the Republic, banned all Uyghur organisations supporting the Uyghur movement and restricted Uyghur press in the Republic.[24] The Joint Statement of 2004 (signed between China and Uzbekistan) was a major success for China, in which both countries agreed that the 'crackdown on the terrorist force of Eastern Turkistan is a major part of the international anti-terrorism campaign'.[25] Unlike Uzbekistan, Uyghurs in Kazakhstan and Kyrgyzstan can establish political organisations.[26]

Apart from bilateral initiatives, China has also used the SCO platform to 'pressure the Central Asian states to control and suppress the activities of "separatist" elements among the significant Uighur diaspora population in the region.'[27] Although there was international outcry over the July 2009 violence in Urumqi, the Central Asian governments remained silent.

The economic development of Xinjiang has received special attention since the beginning of the China's Western Development campaign in 2000, which encouraged greater cooperation with the CARs.[28] There are scholars who have argued—'for China, investment in improving road, rail, and telecommunication links between Xinjiang and Central Asia and the lowering of trade barriers carry as much strategic, as purely economic weight. This imperative has been clear since the collapse of the Soviet

23. Tarimi (2004).

24. Ibid.

25. "China, Uzbekistan Issue Joint Statement on Relation" [Online: Web]. Accessed on 2 November 2010, URL: *http://www.china.org.cn/english/international/98328.htm*

26. *op. cit.* no. 18.

27. *op. cit.* no. 1.

28. Ibid.

Union, with Chinese investment in infrastructure both within Xinjiang itself and between the province and the neighbouring Central Asian states a major element of Chinese policy.'[29]

Bilateral Relations

Understanding the individual priorities and needs of the five CARs has helped China to improve its bilateral relations with these republics, strengthening its position in the region. The rich hydrocarbon reserves of Kazakhstan make it one of the most significant countries in the region. Of the three energy rich CARs, it is Kazakhstan, which shares a border with China. It is argued that, 'China's growing involvement in Central Asia, and particularly Kazakhstan, is set to be one of the most significant trends of the next few years.'[30] Sino-Kazakh trade increased from US $6.9 billion in 2005 to US $14.2 billion in 2009 (Table 10.1). Today China's economic engagement with Kazakhstan has extended beyond pipelines to 'acceleration of trans-border trade and environment projects, and in the banking sector.'[31] In 2007, during Chinese President Hu Jintao's visit to Kazakhstan, both sides agreed to take the bilateral trade figures to US $15 billion by 2015,[32] this target has almost been fulfilled. Both sides have taken the relationship to the level of a strategic partnership. The Kazakhstan-China oil pipeline gave the Republic an alternative to the Russian pipeline system. It also connected the eastern and western parts of Kazakhstan by a pipeline, a shortcoming faced by the country ever since independence.

Though Uzbekistan does not share a border with China, it has drawn considerable Chinese attention. Uzbekistan-China bilateral ties have strengthened over the years. Bilateral trade has increased from US $62.7 million in 2001 to US $1.97 billion in 2009 (Table 10.1). During Chinese Premier Wen Jiabao's visit to Uzbekistan in November 2007, both sides signed a Joint Communiqué, which included agreement to 'further enhance bilateral exchanges at various levels, including high-level visits, and

29. *op.cit.* no. 1.

30. Jackson (2009).

31. Sharip (2010).

32. "China, Kazakhstan Sign Joint Communiqué on Promoting Relations, Trade", 18 August 2007, [Online: Web] Accessed on 2 November 2010, URL: *http://news.xinhuanet.com/english/2007-08/18/content_6561247.htm*

deepen pragmatic cooperation in politics, economy, culture and security.'[33] Uzbekistan and China agreed to increase cooperation to tackle terrorism, separatism and extremism and to further promote cooperation in energy, transportation, telecommunications, agriculture, chemical industry, mining and infrastructure, and continue to explore new areas of cooperation (Text of the Joint Communiqué).[34] Uzbekistan's relations with China were further strengthened after the Andijan incident in May 2005, with the deterioration of Uzbekistan's relation with the West, especially the US, the Republic moved closer to China and Russia in its quest to improve its international image abroad.

Turkmenistan after President Niyazov's death has gradually come out of its isolationist policy. Turkmenistan's agreeing to sell gas to China and the completion of the China-Central Asia pipeline reflects the growing closeness between the two countries. Like Kazakhstan, the deepening of Turkmenistan-China relations reduced the Republic's dependence on Russia for transportation of the Republic's gas to the international markets.

Kyrgyzstan and Tajikistan, the two poorest economies in the region have also benefitted from Chinese investment. China has invested in building roads and rail links in these two countries. During Premier Wen Jiabao's November 2010 visit to Tajikistan, both sides signed a Joint Communiqué, which stated that both sides will 'enhance high-level contacts, expand exchanges and cooperation in various fields to fully develop their relations of good-neighborliness, friendship and cooperation.'[35] Both these republics share border with China, making them strategically significant for China.

Central Asia as the Future Area of Competition

Russia, China and the US are the three main external players engaged in the region, each having its own stake to preserve its stronghold in the region. In future, the region would witness more competition among these

33. "China, Uzbekistan Issue Joint Communiqué, Pledging to Enhance Bilateral Ties, Co-op", 4 November 2007 [Online: Web]. Accessed 18 November 2010, URL: *http://news.xinhuanet.com/english/2007-11/04/content_7008018.htm*.

34. Ibid.

35. "China, Tajikistan Sign Joint Communique to Promote Ties, Cooperation", 26 November 2010 [Online: Web]. Accessed 19 January 2011, URL: *http://english.cpc.people.com.cn/66102/7211786.html*.

three players. Initially after independence of these republics, a common ground for Sino-Russia cooperation was keeping the US at bay from the region. The SCO, which has Russia, China and four other CARs (except Turkmenistan) as members, has provided these countries with a common platform for negotiation. The Sino-Russia convergence of interests was strongly reflected at the 2005 Astana Summit that voiced opposition to the continuing presence of US military bases in Central Asia.

Despite their common interests, Russia and China have several divergences on policy in the region. Russia, which has been the traditional player, is apprehensive of China's growing economic influence. In future, the pursuit by China and Russia of their respective economic interests in this region would create rift between the two countries. The completion of the two pipelines by China has shaken Russia's monopoly over the region's pipeline systems. Another difference of view would be on their respective approaches to the SCO as an organisation in future? Russia, unlike China would not prefer to see the SCO emerge as economic grouping fearing Chinese dominance in the group.

Russia is the main defence partner of each of the CARs. Chinese growing military cooperation with the CARs is yet another concern for Russia, intensifying the differences between the two. Joint military exercises between China and CARs and Chinese military aid to these republics reflects Chinese security imperatives in the region. The first joint military exercise between China and CARs was with Kyrgyzstan in 2002, initially the exercises conducted under SCO were bilateral.[36] Sino-Tajikistan and Sino-Kyrgyzstan joint military excersises were held in 2006 in Tajikistan and Kyrgyzstan, respectively.[37] China under the aegis of the SCO has also conducted several multilateral military exercises with the CARs. Multilateral military exercises took place for the first time in 2003 in Kazakhstan and Xinjiang, all SCO members (except Uzbekistan) participated in it.[38] In 2007, two multilateral exercises took place. In May, 'Issyk Kul Anti-Terror-2007' military exercises took place in Kyrgyzstan and in August 'Peace Mission' involving all SCO members was held in Russia. 'Peace Mission 2010' was held in Kazakhstan in September.

36. Peyrouse (2010).

37. Ibid.

38. Ibid.

China has been giving military aid to the CARs. In 2007, China agreed to give US $3 million as loan to Turkmenistan to meet its military needs like equipment and uniforms.[39] There are scholars who have argued that Chinese military loan to Turkmenistan came immediately after the Republic agreed to supply 30 bcm of gas to China, indicating China's apprehension about the Turkmen army's capability to protect the pipelines.[40] During the May 2010 visit of the Chinese Defence Minister to Kazakhstan, he said, 'military-to-military relationship is a key part of overall bilateral relations—exchanges and cooperation between the two militaries were being strengthened across the board, adding that contacts should be deepened further and taken to a new level.'[41]

China gave US $1.5 miilion as aid to the Tajik military in April 2009. Back in 2005, Chinese Defence Minister, Cao Gangchuan visited Tajikistan, this resulted in signing of several agreements like improving military technical cooperation, training of Tajik officers in China, sharing intelligence and experience on security issues, holding joint anti-terrorist exercises, etc. Drawing attention to the growing relations between the two countries, Cao Gangchuan during this visit said that the bilateral relation is 'developing dynamically and military cooperation is an important component of relations between the two countries.'[42]

Several US oil companies have signed contracts with the CARs. The US too is concerned about the growing Chinese economic presence in the region, which could threaten US economic interests in the region. The US concern about China's growing influence in the region is evident from the recent statement by the US Special Envoy for Energy, Richard Morningstar that the US needs 'to develop strategies to compete with China for energy in Central Asia'.[43] Moreover, the US too will not be comfortable with the Chinese military presence in the region.

---

39. Ibid.
40. Ibid.
41. "China, Kazakhstan Seek to Upgrade Military Cooperation" [Online: Web]. May 29, 2010. Accessed on 12 January 2011, URL: *http://en.rian.ru/world/20100529/159212484.html*
42. Roger (2005).
43. Bhadrakumar (2009).

The competition among the players in the region would accentuate, especially when the CARs today are carefully utilising the competition among the various players to bargain the best deal. These republics are no longer silent spectators of the developments in the region, a factor that all the external players are aware.

Implication for India

The well known historical links between India and Central Asia are not reflected adequately in the post Soviet relationship. China's growing influence impinges on India's long-term energy interest. So far, China has moved far ahead of India in the region. In 2005, India's ONGC lost out to China's CNPC to acquire PetroKazakhstan, delivering a major blow to India's energy quest in the region. A major bottleneck that India faces is the absence of direct transport links with the region, a constraint that China does not have. So far, none of the proposed routes connecting India and the CARs has materialised.

There are analysts, however, who have argued for China and India cooperation to link Central Asia and India. For example, a land-cum-pipeline route connecting Ladakh-Xinjiang-Kyrgyzstan-Tajikistan via Kashgar has been recommended. Rajiv Sikri, former Indian diplomat recommends a parallel oil and gas pipeline via Xinjiang, connecting India and Central Asia through Karakoram and Himalaya ranges. He argues: 'Although they [India and China] may be competitors for finite global energy resources, India and China share a larger long-term interest that the energy resources of Eurasia remain available to meet the demand of Asian consumers too, not just those of the West.'[44] India, however, cannot ignore the security problems arising from this route as it passes through the disputed Aksai Chin. Given the present situation, it is difficult to imagine this route materialising in the near future but as a long-term strategy, it is worth exploring this option too.

Conclusion

China's engagement in the region in the last decade has established it as a major player. However, there are issues, which if not addressed can jeopardise China's relation with the CARs. China so far has been successful

44. Sikri (2008).

in gaining support from the governments of these republics. Nevertheless, suspicion about China still exists among the common people. In recent years, there have been protests against China in some republics. For example, China's request to the Kazakh government to permit Chinese farmers to cultivate one million hectares of land in Kazakhstan met with domestic opposition.[45] Such local opposition may not in the near future play any decisive role in government's decisions. However, no government can ignore discontents being nurtured within the society. Chinese migration in Central Asia is yet another issue that can strain Sino-Central Asia relation. About 100,000 Chinese are believed to have moved into Kazakhstan over the years.[46]

The economic aspects of the relationship also carry a potential for friction and tensions with China. The bulk of Chinese import from Central Asia is raw materials and petroleum/natural gas while China primarily exports low priced manufactured good. China in future could face opposition from the CARs because of this trade pattern, a concern that both sides need to address. Nevertheless, China's investments in the energy sector and infrastructure building in the region will play a determining role in strengthening its position in the region.

45. Pannier (2009).

46. Li and Wang (2009).

References

Asian Development Bank (2010). *Key Indicators for Asia and the Pacific*, Country Tables, [Online: Web]. Accessed on 20 March 2011, URL: *www.adb.org/Statistics*

Bhadrakumar, M.K. (2009). "China Resets Terms of Engagement in Central Asia", *Central Asia*, December 24, [Online: Web] Accessed on 12 January 2011, URL: *http://www.atimes.com/atimes/Central_Asia/KL24Ag04.html*

Clarke, Michael (2010). "China's Deepening Ties with Central Asia", 26 May, [Online: Web] Accessed on 15 January 2011, URL: *http://www.businessweek.com/globalbiz/content/may2010/gb20100526_156952.htm*

Dolkun, Isa (2007). "Uyghur Situation in Central Asia Countries", OSCE Human Dimension Implementation Meeting, Warsaw, 24 September-5 October, [Online: Web] Accessed on 12 September 2010, URL: *http://www.osce.org/odhir/27056.*

Jackson, Alexander (2009). "China and Central Asia", 19 May, [Online: Web] Accessed on 14 February 2011, URL: *http://www/turkishweekly.net/print.asp?type=1&id=77297/china-and-central-asia.html*

Khodzhaev, Ablat (2009). "The Central Asian Policy of the People's Republic of China", *China and Eurasia Forum Quarterly* 7(1): 19, February.

Li, Hak Yin and Zhengxu Wang (2009). *Assessing China's Influence in Central Asia: A Dominant Regional Power?*", The University of Nottingham China Policy Institute, July, [Online: Web] Accessed on 14 January 2011, URL: *http://www.nottingham.ac.uk/cpi/documents/briefings/briefing-53-central-asia.pdf*

Pannier, Bruce (2010). "Kazakhstan Mulls China Land Deal", 19 December, [Online: Web] Accessed on 10 November, URL; *http://www.atimes.com/atimes/Central_Asia/KL19Ag01.html*

Peyrouse, Sebastian (2010). "Military Cooperation between China and Central Asia: Breakthrough, Limits, and Prospects", 5 March, [Online: Web] Accessed on 16 February 2011, URL: *http://www.jamestown.org/single/?no_cache=1&tx_ttnews%5Btt_news%5D=36123*

Roger, McDermott (2005). "China Quietly Increases Military Links with Tajikistan", 22 September, [Online: Web] Accessed on 10 October 2010, URL: *http://www.jamestown.org/programs/edm/single/?tx_ttnews%5Btt_news%5D=30885&tx_ttnews%5BbackPid%5D=176&no_cache=1*

Sadykzhan, Ibraimov (2009). "China-Central Asia Trade Relations: Economic and Social Patterns", *China and Eurasia Quarterly* 7(1): 49.

Sharip, Farkhand (2010). "China's Expansionist Policy toward Kazakhstan takes a New Turn", *Eurasia Daily Monitor* 7(209), 17 November, [Online: Web] Accessed on 2 November 2010, URL: *http://www.jamestown.org/single/?no_cache=1&tx_ttnews%5Btt_news%5D=37181*

Sikri, Rajiv (2008). "The Geopolitics of Energy Security and Implications for South and Southeast Asia", Institute of South Asian Studies *(ISAS) Working Paper* No. 37. 11. February.

Tarimi, N.T. (2004). "China-Uzbek Pact Bad News for Uighurs", 30 July, [Online: Web] Accessed on 10 September 2010, URL: *http://www/atimes.com/atimes/Central_Asia/FG30Ag01html*

11 China's Relations with East Asia and Southeast Asia in the Asia-Pacific Setting

Dilip Lahiri

The increase in Chinese assertiveness over the last two years had raised concerns among virtually all Asia-Pacific stakeholders, which include India, as to whether or not China's spectacular rise in recent decades would actually be peaceful and harmonious as has been repeatedly promised by the Chinese. This assertiveness has been on display particularly in 2010 on maritime and territorial issues in the South China sea, as well as in dealings with the US, ASEAN, Japan and India.

Naval incidents have taken place between Chinese vessels, and those of Vietnam, Malaysia, the Philippines, Indonesia, Japan and the US. Chinese declarations of sovereignty over the South China Sea as a 'core interest' at an ASEAN Regional Forum (ARF) Ministerial in Vietnam in July 2010, was challenged by the majority of ARF members. China was enraged at the offer of US Secretary of State Hillary Clinton to assist in multilateral mediation of the dispute. Stubborn Chinese resistance to UN Security Council and ARF action with respect to the Democratic People's Republic of Korea (DPRK) sinking of an Republic of Korea (ROK) corvette led to major US–ROK naval exercises including an US aircraft carrier, in the East China and Yellow Seas, over loud Chinese protests. An US destroyer then visited Vietnam, the country most aggrieved by China's South Sea posturing, followed by high Vietnamese officers visiting an offshore US aircraft carrier. The crisis with Japan near the disputed Senkaku Islands, rapidly escalated by Chinese bluster, was eventually defused by Japan backing down, but stopping well short of the *mea culpa* (my fault, in Latin) demanded by China.

There has also been a Hanoi-led ASEAN pushback against China's unilateral usage of the waters of international rivers such as the Mekong.

There has been much speculation about the reasons for China changing course from its earlier 'charm diplomacy' which had garnered so much goodwill for China in ASEAN over the previous two decades. There is uncertainty as to whether or not this is a miscalculated overreach, and if , to use a Chinese metaphor, China will pull back, having encountered a stone which gave way under its feet while feeling its way across the river. Internal jostling to establish patriotic credentials, with the PLA trying to secure a larger say in policymaking and 40 million Chinese netizens adopting xenophobic positions, have also been put forward in explanation.

Whatever the Chinese motivation, there seems little doubt that, for the present, Asia-Pacific countries have drawn together to resist Chinese bullying, though there is no appetite on any side to push this further towards an attempt at containment of China.

China in the Asia-Pacific

Since the end of the Cold War, China has built up its economic ascendancy in the region, and is today the biggest trading partner of virtually all the Asia-Pacific countries, in most cases importing more than it exports. China is also the largest destination for investments from most countries in the region. Political interactions have expanded, but at a slower pace. China has made substantial headway in chipping away at historic US primacy, but there is still a long way to go.

Chinese Relations with ASEAN Countries

During the Cold War, China posed a direct political-military threat to the non-communist states in Southeast Asia through its support of communist insurgencies. China's diplomatic opening to East and Southeast Asia began with Nixon's visit to China in 1972, China's replacement of Taiwan as a permanent member of the UN Security Council, and the establishment of diplomatic relations with Malaysia, Thailand and the Philippines in 1974-75. Relations with Indonesia were normalised much later in 1990, followed by Singapore and Brunei.

ASEAN countries have sought to develop a complex engagement of China at the political, economic and strategic levels with the hope that Chinese leaders could be persuaded or socialised into conduct that abided by international rules and norms. Such engagement policies were pursued at the same time as indirect or soft balancing which mainly involved persuading other major powers, particularly the United States, to act as counterweights to Chinese regional influence. ASEAN also pursued a general policy of enmeshing other regional great powers, including India, in order to give them a stake in a stable regional order.

Southeast Asia is a region characterised by its differences and variations in attitudes towards China. Maritime Southeast Asia generally welcomes the US presence in the region. In contrast, continental Southeast Asia operates much more under the constraints of close proximity to China, as well as continental geopolitics involving shared boundaries and competing influences, particularly in Indochina and the Myanmar-Thailand-China nexus. At times these countries appear to be gravitating inexorably toward Chinese influence.

Hanoi harbours the most acute threat perception of China which waged war on Vietnam to 'teach it a lesson' after Vietnam's invasion of Cambodia in 1978. Thailand, by contrast, as the Southeast Asian country with the closest strategic relations with China since the late 1970s, followed by Malaysia, reflect the relative success of engagement and accommodation between China and the region.

Since the end of the Cold War, however, the region's main preoccupation with regional security has centred on the challenges posed by a rising China. Firstly, they are wary about the territorial disputes over islands in the South China Sea, which involve China and four Southeast Asian countries. China and Vietnam had clashed over the Spratly reefs in the late 1980s. Beijing alarmed its Southeast Asian neighbours when it laid claim to the whole South China Sea in 1992. Thereafter the Chinese occupied and built structures on reefs claimed by Vietnam and the Philippines in 1992, 1995, and 1999, the latter of which led to diplomatic confrontations and military tensions. Despite the negotiation of a declaration of conduct with ASEAN in 2002, Vietnam and the Philippines in particular continue to be very wary of Chinese encroachment.

Secondly, Southeast Asian states are concerned about the fallout of a potential conflict between the United States and China if Beijing becomes more assertive, or Washington decides to adopt a more aggressive containment policy toward Beijing. They particularly worry about a conflict over Taiwan, which would destabilise the whole region and force countries to choose sides.

Thirdly, these countries perceive a medium- to long-term threat from regional dominance by the Chinese. This would be most palpable if Beijing pursued aggressive policies in terms of territorial or resource domination. But short of such actions, Southeast Asian countries still remain wary of the potential domination of the regional security and economic landscape by China to the exclusion of other powers, particularly the United States. In this sense, Chinese regional unipolarity *per se* is regarded with suspicion because of uncertainties about Chinese intentions over the long term.

But the main challenge posed by a rising China is economic. China has the second-largest economy after the United States and is still growing strongly. China's economic growth will clearly bring both benefits and costs to Southeast Asia. As the Chinese economy continues to grow, its demand for exports from ASEAN will increase, particularly in terms of primary commodities and natural resources.

China's trade with Southeast Asia grew from $8 billion in 1981 to over $230 billion in 2009. However, this pattern of export led growth, with ASEAN supplying the wherewithal for China's explosive exports of assembled products to the US and EU could obviously not carry on indefinitely. When the dust settles from the recent financial crisis, the character of economic globalisation may be significantly changed with respect to capital flows, production chains and trade patterns.

Southeast Asia also worries about China siphoning off foreign investments in the region: in the last few years, China has been attracting 50 to 70 per cent of the FDI in Asia (excluding from Japan), as opposed to the 20 per cent that ASEAN gets. In addition, Southeast Asia faces stiff Chinese competition in maintaining the competitiveness of its export products in US and EU markets.

Basically China has two key strategic aims in Southeast Asia: first, to ensure that disputes in the sub-region do not compromise Chinese sovereignty, territorial integrity and national security; and second, to ensure that Southeast Asia does not fall within the ambit of another power antagonistic to China (that is the United States or Japan). During the mid-

1990s, Beijing concluded that these aims would best be achieved through positive diplomacy, that is, by first cultivating benign perceptions of China in order to ameliorate Southeast Asian worries about the China threat and to make a concerted effort to represent China's re-emergence as essentially an economic, rather than a strategic development. Under the presidency of Jiang Zemin, China adopted a consciously constructive tone in the key foreign policy aims of 'increasing trust, reducing problems, developing cooperation, and refraining from confrontation.'

China appears to have enjoyed relative success over the last decade in assuaging the worst fears of its Southeast Asian neighbours. As a result, in Southeast Asia there is a notable shift away from perceptions of China as a potentially destabilising force. On the one hand, most policymakers still hold to their realist view that economic capacity will necessarily translate into military might and that sheer capability has the potential to disrupt the region's strategic landscape and deepen their security dilemmas. On the other hand, due to immediate economic advantages of cooperating with China, the same policy elites appear to have become more relaxed about the day-to-day policy implications of China's growth and reconciled themselves to the reality of a resurgent giant.

To be sure, the degree of comfort with the situation varies. Thai officials are quick to assert that they do not regard China as a threat at all, but rather as a crucial market and locomotive of growth for the region. Vietnam, in contrast, is ambivalent toward China because of its history of battling Chinese occupation and because of territorial disputes over islands in the South China Sea.

China-ASEAN Institutionalised Cooperation

Even with formal diplomatic ties, China was fully aware of the suspicion and distrust that lingered among Southeast Asian countries about China. The year 1991 was the turning point in relations between China and ASEAN. The Chinese Foreign Minister was invited to the opening session of the 24th ASEAN Ministerial Meeting in Kuala Lumpur as an observer. With the establishment of a Joint Economic and Trade Committee and a Joint Science and Technology Committee, economic and trade relations between China and ASEAN countries developed rapidly. At the political level, the noteworthy development was the institution of a consultative mechanism between senior officials of the two sides. In 1996, the status of China-ASEAN relations was upgraded from consultative partnership to full dialogue partnership. In 1997, Chinese President Jiang Zemin attended the first China-ASEAN Summit (ASEAN + 1) and an ASEAN-China, Japan and Korea Summit (ASEAN+3). The following year the two sides set up the overall structure of ASEAN-China dialogue mechanisms, composed of five committees and the ASEAN-China Cooperation Fund.

During the 1997-98 Asian financial crisis, China decided not to devalue its currency in order to help other Southeast Asian countries handle their economic downturn. Later it actively participated in the Chiangmai Initiative and other financial arrangements, though these were never put to the test. As part of the responses to the crisis, a China-ASEAN free trade area (FTA) was proposed. In 2001, the China ASEAN Summit decided to establish the FTA within 10 years and signed the China-ASEAN Framework Agreement on Comprehensive Economic Cooperation.

On the political side, China and ASEAN in 2002 adopted the Declaration on the Conduct of Parties in the South China Sea, by which the parties undertook to exercise self-restraint in the conduct of activities that could complicate or escalate disputes and affect peace and stability in the region and to handle their differences in a constructive manner. Following that, security dialogues between defence officials and think tanks were held. In 2003, China acceded to the Treaty of Amity and Cooperation in Southeast Asia and its two Protocols. That year, during the Bali Summit, leaders of China and ASEAN adopted a Joint Declaration on Strategic Partnership for Peace and Prosperity. In the following years, under the Plan of Action for the Declaration for 2005-2010, a large array of programmes and projects of cooperation were carried out relating to foreign affairs, economy, transport, customs, law, youth affairs, public health, telecommunications, information, quality supervision and combating transnational crimes.

In 2008, the trade volume between China and ASEAN had reached US $231.12 billion, composing 9 per cent of China's total trade volume, almost 30 times the trade volume in 1991. In terms of investment, the actual investment from ASEAN to China has reached US $52 billion while Chinese enterprises have invested a relatively modest US $6.1 billion in ASEAN countries until 2008.

The Asia-Pacific Regional Security Architecture

At the time of establishment of the East Asian Summit (EAS), with the inclusion of India, Australia and New Zealand, China ensured that the ASEAN+3 (China, Japan and ROK) would remain at the heart of ASEAN policymaking on regional cooperation as a price for the dilution of its voice in the EAS. The ASEAN+3 has come a long way over the years and retains considerable brand equity among ASEAN countries which benefitted the most from China's markets during the financial crisis.

But the regional security architecture looks set for rebalancing in ways favouring broader inclusivity and for expanding into new areas of cooperation. ASEAN decided recently to let in the US and Russia into the EAS. The first ever meeting of the ASEAN defence ministers and their eight dialogue counterparts (ASEAN+8 composition) took place in Hanoi on October 12, 2010. Later that month, the East Asia Summit (EAS) convened with Secretary Clinton and Russian Foreign Minister Lavrov attending. This set the stage for the United States (and Russia)to join this 16-member grouping, and for President Obama to attend the 2011 EAS meeting in Jakarta. The emergence of the EAS in its new avatar will dilute the ASEAN+3 process (China, Japan and South Korea) that has been China's preferred forum.

China's Relations with Japan

The People's Republic of China (PRC) and Japan normalised diplomatic relations in 1972. Normalisation took place in the wake of the the 1971 Nixon shock and America's decision to seek rapprochement with China without prior consultation with Japan.

Until the early 1990s, Sino-Japanese relations were conducted within the so-called framework of 'friendship diplomacy', which was centred on deepening bilateral economic ties through trade and investment, and Japan's extension from 1979 of Official Development Assistance (ODA) to China.

Deep historical distrust remains, however, more than 100 years after Japan annexed Taiwan from the Qing Dynasty, and later, in the early 1930s, invaded and occupied much of China. Anti-Japan sentiment is easily whipped up in China. For its part, in Japan, public image of China has steadily turned unfavourable.

Although the post-Cold War period has seen booming bilateral economic interactions, the relations between Tokyo and Beijing in the politico-military area have become progressively tense, deteriorating to unprecedented levels during the administration of Japanese Prime Minister Koizumi Junichiro (2001-2006), but improving in the post-Koizumi era till the recent maritime incident.

China's market is very important for Japan. China is Japan's biggest two-way trading partner. Japanese companies generated $382 billion in sales there last year, according to trade ministry data. Three of China's top-selling car brands this year are Japanese. The relationship of course goes both ways. Japan is the third-largest source of foreign direct investment into China. Beijing needs that capital and technology to maintain growth. The economic relationship has proved durable despite a long history of animosity. Even in 2005, when relations were last at their nadir—and when stone-throwing protesters broke windows at Tokyo's embassy in Beijing—Japanese investment into China hit a record.

Following the demise of the Soviet Union and the end of bipolarity, Japan and China were confronted with a new strategic environment in East Asia. In particular, profound differences emerged between the two neighbours regarding their respective views of the US regional role.

The shift in the relative balance of power between the two has contributed to the exacerbation of mutual distrust. While for Japan, the 1990s was a period of economic slowdown, for China it was a decade of rapid economic growth, which continued into the 2000s. China has already overtaken Japan in terms of nominal GDP. Japan's regional leadership has been undermined by its stagnant economy in the 1990s and perceived inability to deal satisfactorily with the Asian financial crisis, which contrasted with Beijing's behaviour as a 'responsible power' during the crisis. In 2004, the PRC replaced the US as Japan's largest trading partner. With its economic stagnation, Japan progressively lost confidence that it could handle relations with China on its own through ODA etc., and started looking for potential allies with converging interests. Japan discontinued bilateral ODA to China after the Beijing Olympics.

Mutual concerns regarding strengthened military postures and suspicion regarding one another's long-term strategic goals in East Asia

have emerged as defining characteristics of Sino-Japanese relations. While Tokyo has concluded that China's primary goal in the foreseeable future is to attain military superiority in a situation of potential conflict over Taiwan, Japan is worried that China's rapid development and deployment since the mid-1990s of short- and intermediate-range missiles has increased its ability to strike not only Taiwan, but also Japan and some of the main US military bases in East Asia, raising questions about the reliability of US extended deterrence.

China's expansion of its naval and air military capabilities has also raised concerns in Tokyo as this would allow Beijing to project power into the East and South China Sea which are vital for Japan's sea lanes of communication (SLOC). The ongoing territorial dispute over the Senkaku/Diaoyu Islands is representative of a mounting Sino-Japanese energy rivalry, as there are prospects for large oil and gas reserves in the surrounding waters. The dispute escalated in 2004 amid revelations of China's development of a natural gas project very close to the Japan-drawn demarcation line of the contested exclusive economic zone (EEZ) border in the East China Sea. In 2008, the two sides later inked an agreement on the joint exploration of a disputed gasfield in the East China Sea.

China's view of Japan's changing security posture since the 1990s has mirrored Tokyo's mistrust toward Beijing. China has repeatedly expressed worries regarding Japan's re-emergence as a major military power, emphasising Tokyo's drive to acquire new military capabilities, notably ballistic missile defence (BMD) systems, and its expansion of the self-defence forces (SDFs) missions. The Taiwan question that led Beijing to see Tokyo's adjustments in its security policy through the lens of cross-Strait relations.

From a Japanese perspective, the perceived North Korean military threat is a legitimate reason to strengthen its defence posture and alliance with the US. China has been worrying that the revised 1997 US-Japan Defence Guidelines could be applied to a conflict relating to Taiwan, as Tokyo and Washington have refused to explicitly rule Taiwan in or out of envisaged contingencies. According to some Chinese analysts, inclusion of Taiwan in the US-Japan security cooperation 'serves to embolden the separatist forces in Taiwan'. Beijing's fears were heightened in 2005 when a

joint US-Japan statement indicated the 'peaceful resolution' of the Taiwan Strait issue as one of their 'common strategic objectives' in the Asia-Pacific region.

Changes in both countries' domestic politics provided the context in the first half of the 2000s for increased mutual animosity, by allowing the main bilateral problems, notably the interpretation of history, territorial disputes and the Taiwan question, to dominate the Sino-Japanese agenda. While persistent historical grievances on the Chinese side were a major destabilising factor in the relations, the conservative trend in Japanese domestic politics provided a fertile ground for the rise of mutually hostile nationalistic sentiments. Feelings of public animosity towards Japan exploded in China in 2001 and 2005 in the wake of the Japanese Ministry of Education's approval of history textbooks for middle schools written by a right-wing group of nationalistic scholars. Added to this were Koizumi's yearly pilgrimages to the Yasukuni Shrine. The history issue was also the root cause of the large-scale anti-Japan demonstrations throughout China in the spring of 2005 in the wake of Tokyo's renewed bid for a permanent seat on the UNSC.

Sino-Japanese security relations have been conducted largely within a triangular framework of interactions with the US. America's military presence in East Asia and role as a provider for regional stability has been a crucial determinant of Japanese and Chinese respective security policies. For Tokyo, its alliance with the US is the bedrock of Japan's national security. For Beijing, the US (and its strengthened security partnership with Japan) poses the greatest potential threat to Beijing's internal stability and leadership ambitions in East Asia. What mostly concerns Beijing is the perceived US hegemony in East Asia, of which Tokyo is seen as a main pillar, and its impact on the Taiwan issue. On the other hand, China continues to recognise the usefulness of the US security umbrella for putting a cap on Japan's rearmament.

China-Korea Relations

South Korea and China bilateral trade and people-to-people contacts have grown spectacularly since diplomatic relations were established in 1992. China has been the number one trade partner to South Korea since

2003, overtaking the United States. More than 20,000 South Korean firms have invested in China in the past 20 years. South Korea's cumulative foreign direct investment (FDI) in China accounted for 21 per cent of China's total FDI, standing at $29.3 billion as of 2010. 66,806 South Koreans studied in China in 2009, almost equal to the number of South Korean students in the United States. Seven out of 10 of the 76,000 foreign students studying in ROK are Chinese. South Korean pop culture has swept Japan, China and Southeast Asia, in a phenomenon called 'Hallyu,', a term coined in mid-1999 by Chinese journalists surprised by the rapid growth in popularity of South Korean entertainment and goods in China.

However, North Korea remains a thorn in South Korea's relations with China. China's reaction to the warship Cheonan's sinking has been cause for deep anger inside South Korea. In the initial days after the incident, China made little reference to the loss of life. More offensive was the invitation to Kim Jong-Il to visit Beijing in the midst of the tensions. When ROK President Lee visited Shanghai on April 30, China's president, Hu Jintao did not agree to support a regional response to the incident. ROK is angry with China for preventing the naming of DPRK in the UN Security Council in June 2010 as responsible for the sinking of the Cheonan. Later China objected strongly to the large-scale joint naval exercises conducted by the US and ROK in the East China and Yellow seas to warn DPRK against further adventurism.

ROK's close military alliance with the US and the presence of 30,000 odd US troops in ROK is also a constant backdrop to bilateral relations. The two countries have different approaches to Korean unification and the future orientation of the Peninsula. There is also latent concern in ROK about China's economic rise and growing self-confidence encouraging elements within China's political security apparatus to become more aggressive in pursuing its core interests.

China-DPRK Relations

China has been widely recognised for over four decades as North Korea's closest patron. It has served as a conduit for DPRK's communication with major regional powers, a political and diplomatic protector, and an indispensable source of economic support. The strategic glue binding

the two countries has been the 'Sino-North Korean Treaty of Friendship, Cooperation and Mutual Assistance' of 1961.

However, since its reform and open-door policy in 1978, China has pursued a different set of strategies and directions for its national development, resulting in a widening gap between its national interests and those of North Korea. The Sino-North Korean alliance has been redefined from its earlier characterisation to 'lips-to-teeth', to an alliance of asymmetrical interdependence.

Signs of future changes in their relationship include China's active and immediate diplomatic involvement in dealing with North Korea's renewed nuclear push since 2003 and unusually public academic arguments in China for the redefinition of the Sino-North Korean alliance. Despite its periodic exasperation with DPRK, however, there are no signs that its value to China has depreciated to a point where China will let it sink. On its part, the DPRK has skillfully leveraged this factor in its relations with the US and its handling of the nuclear weapons issue through the Six Party talks.

China-Australia Relations

In the wake of the Australian election on August 21, 2010, a heated debate has opened up in the press over the emergence of China as a major power, growing US-China rivalry in the region and its implications for Canberra's strategic orientation into the future. For Australia, rising regional tensions present a fundamental dilemma: how to balance between China, which is now Australia's largest trading partner, and the United States, which has been the cornerstone of strategic and defence policy since World War II. Washington's increasingly assertive pushback against Beijing was undoubtedly a major factor in this controversy.

Statements by the Australian Foreign Minister indicate that, for the present, Australia will continue to accord primacy to its strategic and military alliance relationship with the US and its continuing presence in the Asia-Pacific, and to compartmentalise these from its increasingly overwhelming trade and investment relationship with China. However, the very fact that suggestions are being made by mainstream analysts that Australia may have to resign itself to tugging its forelock in adjusting to Chinese ascendancy in the region is perhaps a straw in the wind. While

Australia is normally at pains to avoid the impression of bending to Chinese pressure, it would be recalled that Australia was quick to distance itself from the Australia-Japan-India US 'quadrilateral' after a Chinese reprimand.

The US in the Asia-Pacific

In geostrategic terms, the US has traditionally maintained primacy in East Asia based on its capacity to exert 'sea control' over the Western Pacific, both through the naval assets of its Pacific fleet and its network of 'hub and spokes' military alliances with Japan, ROK and several ASEAN countries. The security relations of most Asian countries with China have been largely conducted within a triangular framework of interactions with the US. The US military presence in East Asia and role as a provider for regional stability has been a crucial determinant of the hedging strategies towards China followed in greater or lesser measure by all countries in the region.

Nixon's visit to China in 1972 initiated a period during which US strategic primacy in Asia ceased to be opposed actively by China. Over the last 15 years, the economic foundations and military dimensions of US primacy in Asia have been significantly eroded as China's economy has grown. This is expected to continue in coming years. As the economic foundation of the United States' primacy erodes, the Asian order that has been built on it can be expected to change. China will inevitably aim for a wider leadership role in Asia.

Much will depend on how the United States responds to China's rise. A US decision to contest China's challenge would inevitably increase strategic competition between them. China would then either have to forgo aspirations to lead Asia itself and accept that the United States will remain a major player and constraint on China's freedom of action. As a corollary, it may perhaps also have to accept Japan as a major participant in Asia's strategic affairs.

Alternatively, the United States could elect to share power with China and proceed along the road of Obama's first visit to China with the talk of G-2 and all that it entails. The stronger Beijing becomes, and the more important to Washington it grows, the less sure Tokyo can be that Washington will always put Japanese interests ahead of Beijing's.

Like Japan, the United States' other allies in Asia will face hard choices in handling the geostrategic implications of China's rise. Australia's economy is already in thrall to China's market. They would need to decide whether Australia should support the United States in contesting China's predominance, or slide towards an uneasy and insecure neutrality. For most ASEAN countries, an open US–China contest would end the circumstances which have allowed them to follow an independent path.

For the present, the US appears to have decided to maneuver towards retaining its primacy. Secretary of State, Hilary Clinton (2009), said recently, 'The United States is not ceding the Pacific to anyone.' There also appears to be emerging a sort of regional strategic consensus *vis-à-vis* China that welcomes greater engagement on the part of the United States in the political and economic as well as military realms in the Asia-Pacific.

India's Role in East and Southeast Asia

Over the past 18 years, India has made a concerted effort to direct its foreign, economic and defence policies eastward through its 'Look East' policy. India is generally recognised today as having an important footprint in matters relating to Asia-Pacific regional economic and security stability. While India also wants cooperative and mutually beneficial relations with China, it would be deeply uncomfortable with a Sinocentric order in East Asia, and is closely interested in ensuring that China's rise does not take this form.

India's eastward focus began in the economic sphere in 1991 with attempts to link its own liberalising economy to the dynamic 'tigers' of Southeast Asia. This was around the same time as the opening of China's relations with ASEAN. This process for India has been slow and sometimes halting. But India has recently signed a free trade agreement with ASEAN amid burgeoning trade and investment relations with ASEAN countries.

These economic linkages led to military cooperation initially with countries such as Singapore, Vietnam and Indonesia which saw India as, in the words of Singaporean senior minister-mentor Lee Kuan Yew, 'a useful balance to China's heft' in the framework of the ASEAN policy or trying to enmesh all major powers in the region's affairs. Such cooperation now extends to India's strategic partnerships and defence cooperation with Japan,

Australia and ROK, apart from the 40 joint military exercises with the US since 2001, including one of the largest multilateral naval exercises ever held in the region, Malabar 2007, which featured three aircraft carriers, 28 surface vessels and 150 aircraft from India, the US, Japan, Australia and Singapore.

India is comfortably situated with respect to the expected future consolidation of the regional architecture around the EAS. The advantage of EAS is that ASEAN is comfortable with it as they would still remain in the driver's seat. India's dialogue partner status with ASEAN and membership of ARF before China was more due to the push by ASEAN and ASEAN +3 members like Singapore, Indonesia and Japan than an accomplishment of Indian diplomacy. Their intention was to balance China in the indirect ASEAN style. It is important for India to nurture this constituency. In due course, India will also be able to enter APEC, the only major Asia-Pacific forum of which India is still an outsider. But the key to becoming a real East Asian insider will be the substantive contribution India can make to the deliberations in these fora.

12 China and the International System

Madhu Bhalla

It is striking that in Chinese foreign policy documents or leadership speeches from Mao onwards, forms a continuous thread. One sees this in Mao's 'three world' concept, in Deng Xiaoping's speech at the United Nations General Assembly in which he elaborated this concept and again in Hu Jintao's 2003 enunciation of the 'harmonious world' concept. In 2004 and 2006, Hu Jintao once again provided an elaborate analysis of the international system in which he basically extended the harmonious world concept. All these statements are very specific in locating China's foreign policy within the international system. These analyses are very dialectical, full of contradictions, not laid out in absolute terms and heavily contextualised, and the sense is of a very complex picture of the world at any time during which Chinese foreign policy has been defined.

The most relevant and current analysis is that of Hu Jintao. This was reiterated as late as in 2009 at the 11th Ambassadorial Conference that was held in Beijing. The significant point in Hu's exposition is the continuity with and extension of Deng Xiaoping's concepts. He added to the 'harmonious world' concept in the sense that he provided room for using soft power as a political tool for expansion of China's political influence. Secondly, he exhorted the diplomats who were at the conference to be more active on specific issues, related to China's national sovereignty, rather than be preoccupied in a general manner with diplomacy. If one compares this with his advice to the diplomats in July 2009, one can see the linkage with China's increased assertiveness over the last year over specific issues—especially territorial.

He also talked about multilateralism, multipolarity and the decline of unilateralism. So, what he said was actually a combination of all of the crucial issues that China has been talking about for some time, as well as the addition of a more assertive and outgoing approach to the world. This is partly related to the US being affected by the global financial crisis, and the Chinese assessment that they have come up in the world, relative to the US, and that they need to be much more assertive in the international system. Whether they want to take a leadership position on this is something that is still being actively debated in China, precisely because the Chinese are not quite sure whether they have the capability to extend themselves globally, but certainly within the region and on a few global issues, the Chinese are willing and capable to extend themselves and take on more of a leadership role. Much of this is not very clear within Chinese foreign policymaking circles and some of the debates that are most articulate, still centre around the exhortation of Deng Xiaoping, 'Keep your head low, don't take leadership positions.' Thus, the debate on China's profile continues, but overall there is a sense that China now feels it should take a more prominent position in the international system.

The question is what kind of leadership role within the international system. Is China going to be a revisionist power, or is it going to rewrite the rules of the international system. It is interesting that at the Ambassadorial Conference, there was a consensus on multilateralism and on deeper and wider multilateral involvement. There was no debate on that, the debate was on whether to take a leadership position or continue to keep your head low. There was a consensus that China has to be involved across the board in all multilateral groupings. This view was qualified with the idea that it would be a gradual process because the more important aspect of Chinese foreign policy was its sets of bilateral and trilateral relationships, including those with local regional powers. So, what was suggested was gradualism in its multilateral approach, and involvement in multilateral processes i.e., the new approach would be built upon a traditional form of foreign policy-making. This is an important point.

If we look at some of the events that took place over the last year in terms of what the China defined as its involvement in multilateral fora or processes, we find that out of, say, 10 events, 1 or at most 2, were truly multilateral. The rest were actually bilateral or unilateral actions on the part of China. So, there is some confusion among Chinese policy-makers on what constitutes multilateral involvement and what is truly just still bilateral involvement within a multilateral forum. In the 2009 ambassadorial meeting, China also defined for itself, certain challenges that the country would face in the future. Many of these are familiar, and none seem very new. The first challenge is maintaining a stable relationship with the United States. So, despite the understanding that US was declining as a hegemon power, and unilateralism would at some point decline to be an effective force, the fact is that the US still plays the most important role for the Chinese. The second most important thing was to sustain China's economic growth, because upon that rests the stability and indeed the survival of the regime. Thirdly, to maintain peace and stability in the region, and if possible globally. Keep its periphery stable, be a responsible stakeholder in the global economy and regional security, support and work for reform in the global financial system, support the momentum towards multipolarity, involve oneself in multilateral institutions, deal with domestic challenges and non-traditional security, use soft power as an instrument of political change and move from defensive and passive diplomacy to more proactive diplomacy. These were new elements in the approach outlined in 2009.

The milieu in which China has had to face these challenges has many positive elements. The first element as China sees it, is a shift in the power structure, both in the region and globally. This is something that China calls a very narrow strategic opportunity. Therefore, it is anxious to take advantage of this strategic wind of opportunity by pushing ahead economic reforms that will deal with economic inequalities at home and other domestic economic problems as well as allow the Chinese economy to deal with the economic recession while keeping the external environment stable. Both these are priorities as far as the Chinese are concerned because this window of opportunity is narrow and will not last very long. The Chinese assessment seems to be that the situation is in flux, but at some point it will stabilise. But before that happens, the Chinese need to take advantage of the strategic window of opportunity.

Current Chinese strategic analyses indicate a sense of urgency and a perception of wide ranging threats to security, traditional and non-traditional. The Chinese also seem acutely aware that in a globalised world while the critical issues that may create instability are domestic ones, the trigger often comes from abroad i.e., there is a link between the domestic situation and their domestic turmoil and the globalised environment. They have seen this in the case of Tibet, in Xinjiang, and the way the West has pressured them on various issues particularly human rights. All this could actually detract from China's image which is very important for China today as a rule making power in global and multilateral institutions and also because this is a time when China is seeking to use its soft power and moral suasion. It could also actually encourage a groundswell of domestic dissent leading to internal conflict, or alternatively a nationalistic demand for a confrontational foreign policy. And all these aspects are extremely critical as far as China's objective of creating economic growth at home and stability abroad are concerned, whether these factors operate singly or whether they converge.

Therefore, there is within Chinese foreign policymaking thinking a 'disintegration syndrome', which applies to many areas of foreign and security policy, notably Taiwan. If China fails to unify Taiwan and this is their ultimate goal, it will set in motion a domino effect with major and minor minority groups and regions within China seceding from the state or seeking to secede. This is the worst case scenario, but Chinese policy-makers and analysts talk about it. However, and there is also a positive aspect, i.e., globalisation has also contributed to China's economic success and to its embeddedness in the region. This is important because the embeddedness allows the major powers to safeguard China from the worst effects of big power hostility.

There is yet another aspect which China is increasingly seeking to take advantage of in a positive sense. China's economic status and political influence at a period of system change also encourages the developing world to look to it to support their interests in multilateral institutions. So, China has a huge constituency out there in the developing world, which sees the emergence of a specific Chinese way of looking at multilateral associations and practices as a combination of pragmatism with values that are not western dominated and this makes the Chinese perspective on multilateralism extremely attractive especially to nations in Africa and some nations in Southeast Asia (Myanmar is a good example). In the interim we also find that so far it is the western world which has come up with the norms and values and conventions in multilateralism, and suddenly with Hu Jintao's 'harmonious world' concepts, this is being actively put forward as a guiding principle for a new world order based on Chinese principles. This is perhaps a coup for the Chinese. The language of the 'harmonious world' concept stands in contrast to the realpolitik assumptions of a state of anarchy; it also indicates a tolerance for 'pluralism' at the global level and democratisation of the international system, all of which go down well with developing nations. The concept also responds to fears of China's rise and seeks to provide what Chinese analysts call 'public goods', an alternative theoretical vision to international society. This is the first time after Mao that China had actually tried to put forth a vision for the world.

What are the strengths and weaknesses that China brings to this task? This is how China actually has begun to be able to formulate its vision of what it needs to do and how the international system needs to change and the direction in which it seeks to change the international system, rewrite the rules as and when it has the opportunity. This paper outlines some of the principal strengths of China particularly its rapid economic growth. This ensures China a place at the high table and recognition that no issue can be resolved without China being part of the solution. (It could be of course part of the problem but it definitely has to be brought in at the time of solution.) It also creates ability as far as China is concerned to use its economic clout to effect results. It has just done that with Japan and it will likely do that with other states as well. It used its economic clout on the boycott of the Olympics and it will certainly use its economic clout and its political influence to have a lot of states not go to the Nobel ceremony in Stockholm.

Secondly, globalisation has had an impact on China's relations with the EU, the US, Southeast Asia, Latin America, Africa. This is a truly global policy but crafted bilaterally and it is noteworthy that it actually puts China into the global sphere but these are bilateral arrangements that China has made and which have worked to China's advantage. It is expanding military power because its reach is limited but it can keep the borders secured from local threats. So, it has a limited purpose but this limited purpose is critical for China's regional stability. It is also relevant that in Southeast Asia and East Asia, China has enormous soft power. This goes a long way in actually persuading many people who doubt China or who fear China's rise, from actually taking action against China or at least rationalising Chinese conduct often in positive vein.

But China also has many weaknesses. The contentions within China's political system could vitiate China's communication with the outside world, and could be at the root of the China threat, the China fear syndrome that has emerged. It does not as yet have the capabilities to ensure its interests abroad for example. It is also vulnerable to threats such as piracy; it has a large number of territorial problems on its borders which keep it focussed on this goal. China's multilateralism is limited and uncompromising. In the United Nations where it is a power in the P5, it is fully multilateral. In the SCO where it has leadership it is completely multilateral; in other organisations for example in the G-8 or in the G-28 where it has to share power and authority with other states, it is selectively multilateral. So, China's multilateralism is not as wide as it could be, it does not involve China as much as it could, but what that means essentially is that China will seek to change multilateral organisations so that it can be effectively multilateral in time to come. Of course domestic issues of development, the ambivalence of partial power, mean that China does not have complete full power as a rising and a major state.

China has a fair amount of successes in the way in which it manages its relationship with the United States. It beats any linear logic about the success or the meaning of a relationship that you can imagine. It is a very complicated an ambivalent relationship, one which has seen standoffs and yet it is a totally interdependent relationship. In the neighbourhood it is generally positive, because East Asia and the environment is generally positive for the moment, although in the last year or so it has seen a lot of tensions. But the neighbourhood does not actually threaten China in any way. It is not the neighbourhood, it is not the periphery, or America that will actually change China's assessments of the international system, it is what China does in multilateral processes and in multilateral institutions that is the key issue.

13 China and South Asia

Sreemati Chakrabarti

This paper is focussed on 'China's Soft Power in South Asia'. The Confucius Institutes being the case study. The term 'soft power' was popularised by Harvard Professor Joseph Nye in a book published in 1990. He developed the concept further in 2004 in a second well known book titled: *Soft Power: The Means to Success in World Politics*. It has come to be used extensively by strategists, diplomats, academics, and even political leaders. Soft power may be defined as the means by which one is able to obtain what one desires through co-option and attraction as opposed to hard power where there is coercion. The primary currencies of soft power that a state has at its disposal values, institutions, culture and its domestic policies. While many scholars put economic aid, business, trade and investment as components of soft power, those aspects will not be considered in this paper, as all of them have a hard character; i.e., apply economic sanctions and hurt somebody.

The use of soft power to control and subdue others has been used by colonial powers since the beginning of the modern era. Religion has been used by imperialist powers for spreading their influence. The role of missionaries all over the non-Christian world is too well known to be documented here. Equally significant has been the use of the language of the colonial powers to bring the colonised under their control. The Spaniards, the French, the Japanese and the British as well as others had devised both coercive and persuasive methods to impose their language on subdued peoples. It is noteworthy, however, that the outcomes of colonial language policies have been varied.

In the post-World War II era, American soft power has been nearly as influential as its hard power. No one can deny that even at the height of the Cold War, American ideas and values, culture, education and the political system attracted a large number of elites, even from the countries which opposed US foreign policy. American universities had large numbers of students from Eastern Europe, Egypt, Palestine and India among others.

With the success of its economic reforms, China has been on a massive image building exercise; it prefers to go ahead through the 'soft power' route. Aware of its destabilising influence in the earlier decades of the People's Republic, i.e., the pre-reform era, as well as the intense and deep-rooted soft power of the United States, China has adopted what Kurlantzick (2007) has called a 'charm offensive' as an integral part of its foreign policy. Use of its diplomatic and cultural power has first been evident in Southeast Asia, and now is being increasingly seen in Latin America and Africa as well. China's soft power is expressed mainly through the following measures in the developing world, i.e., cultural exchanges, sending doctors, teachers and students, inviting students and scholars, and paying for Chinese language programmes. According to Esther Pan (2006), these are done with three purposes, one, to convince the world of its peaceful intentions; two, secure resources to fuel its economic growth and, three, to isolate Taiwan.

As with the case of hard power globally, China has to counter and offset America's soft power impact. The influence of American culture and ideas in the form of Hollywood movies, pop music, fast food chains, fashion, attire etc., not only in the developing world but also in China itself is too profound to be neutralised within the next few decades of this century. For the educated well-off urban youth all over the world, the USA is seen as the leading trendsetter in fashion, verbal communication and many other aspects of modern living. In the area of education and science and technology to the soft power that the US wields even now is unmatched by any country. Common knowledge tells us that for students all over the world, the most favoured destination for higher education in almost all disciplines is the United States of America. How China can make inroads into this American influence on the rest of the world is difficult to estimate.

In South Asia, it is India's soft power which China will have to deal with. Not just Bollywood films and songs and television soap operas, but the hold of India's civilisational attributes are too deep-rooted in most of the South Asian countries for China to make inroads into. Language, religion, food and elite culture in which I include literature, dance, music, theatre, etc., of India have an intense influence on all our South Asian neighbours despite our uneasy political relations with them—or rather our love/hate relationship with them. Today's South Asian nation states—Pakistan, Bangladesh, Nepal, Bhutan and Sri Lanka—have all been within the Indian civilisational area. Writing on the issue of China's soft power in South Asia, Parama Sinha Palit (2011) says the following: 'Contemporary Chinese foreign policy, both at the global as well as the regional level, is distinct in its attempt to portray China as a peace-loving, cooperative, tolerant, confident, and responsible power. Beijing is confident that soft power diplomacy will not only enhance its global status but it will also ensure peace and stability in the neighbourhood and encourage economic development. However, the conscious encouragement of the "soft" component in its foreign policy does not imply a concomitant dilution of the hard segment.'

Indeed, China's foreign policy strategy in South Asia is a pertinent example of its judicious balance between soft and hard strategies. At the same time, the deployment of soft and hard power in the region have distinct country-specific applications. The application of soft power appears to be more intense in the relatively smaller countries of South Asia as compared to India, which is not only the largest South Asian country but is also the most strategically critical entity at the South Asian systemic level. China's overall foreign policy strategy for South Asia may be categorised into India and non-India categories with a varying mix of 'hard' and 'soft' power.

Chinese leaders as well as the Chinese media have in the recent past made their own assessment of China's soft power potential. President Hu Jintao as early as 2003 had stated that China's peaceful development strategy would be implemented in its neighbourhood by deploying soft power. Wen Jiabao delivering the Government Work Report on March 5, 2010 said that China would attach more importance to cultural development and conduct cultural exchanges with foreign countries more actively so as to enhance the influence of Chinese culture. *Peoples' Daily* reported that at the sessions of the last National People's Congress (NPC) and Chinese People's Political Consultative Conference (CPPCC) very recently, soft power had become the key word.

A new tool in China's cultural diplomacy is the establishment of Confucius Institutes. It is one of most watched efforts in promoting Chinese soft power. Called the Chinese version of the British Council, their main aim is to promote the learning of the Chinese language, and acquiring knowledge on Chinese culture. Set up in 2004, there are now more than 200 of them spread all over the world. This figure is something that I have put in as part of some guess work because I got different figures in different places between 100 and 500. So, after reading a few more documents I came to the conclusion there are roughly 200 of them. The Confucius Institutes provide Chinese language programmes at various levels, offer training for Chinese teachers, administer exams and tutor services in Chinese and also organise competitions. A few also offer consultancy services for studying in China and provide commercial information regarding China. The Confucius Institutes are funded partly by the Han Pan i.e., the China National Office for Teaching Chinese as Foreign Language and are jointly managed by Chinese universities and foreign parties, i.e., the university in the host country. About US $37 million is spent by the Chinese government on the Confucius Institutes and the teaching of Chinese language around the world. This is not a very significant sum compared to the £5 billion which the British Council spends each year.

Taking into account the widespread mushrooming of Confucius Institutes all over the world, their existence in South Asia is nominal, as is indicated by the following distribution: Afghanistan has one in Kabul University; Bangladesh has one in the North South University, which is a private university; Nepal has one in Kathmandu University; Pakistan has one in the National University of Modern Languages in Rawalpindi; Sri Lanka has one in Kelaniya University; Bhutan and Maldives have not set up Confucius Institutes as yet. Regarding India, it could be said that we have almost no functioning Confucius Institutes. The centre in JNU never got going; but the one at the Vellore Institute of Technology has started holding classes this year. The relatively small number of Confucius Institutes in India contrasts with the numbers in some other countries. Australia has 9; Canada 7; France 8; Germany, Japan, Russia, have 11 each; Italy has 9; South Korea 13; the UK 14 and the United States 46.

It is instructive to look at a functioning example of a Confucius Institute in our region i.e., the one at Kathmandu University. It was set up in 2007 on the campus of the University. It is part of the University, but it is not located in the main campus, but in a place called Balkumari, about 30 km away from the city and housed in the School of Business Management. (This location, is a tactful move.) This Confucius Institute has five faculty members including one Director who heads it; one counted three classrooms and they hold only part time classes. Mostly held early morning, late afternoon or evening so that people who are working can take advantage of this. The Director and teachers are all Chinese.

Its stated aim is to strengthen bilateral relations in the realm of education, culture and tourism. It is supplemented by a China Study Centre in Jhapa in Eastern Nepal to help local entrepreneurs to do business with China. Most of the people who have graduated from there, enrolled in 2007, and since then, it appears that 25-30 have apparently graduated from there and good number of them were working as interpreters for our conference. Most of them had either learned Chinese in China or were employed with some Chinese firm. They are all hoping to get jobs in these firms, or as interpreters in the tourism industry because the number of Chinese coming to Nepal is increasing in leaps and bounds. It is obvious that such openings are limited, and are essentially seasonal, but these aspirants are happy that they earn some income which is a tiny sum i.e., the 3 to 4 months they work.

There are constraints in the propagation of Chinese language and culture in South Asia. The overall education standards in most of the countries in this region is not high enough to attract students to a foreign language, much less a language like Chinese. India's case is somewhat different i.e., infrastructure-related problems, lack of classrooms and language labs. Another inadequacy is lack of housing for teachers. Hence, teachers in China who are interested in coming to India are discouraged from doing so because of lack of proper housing. Most teachers in the Han Pan in Beijing prefer to go to developed countries. The Director of the Kathmandu Institute said that there were 4-5 very good people. In sum, it is very difficult to find people to come and teach in countries like Nepal and Afghanistan and even more so in Pakistan. Then the other constraint is the India factor which comes out more in informal conversation. Except for Pakistan, all the countries in South Asia are wary that excessive closeness to China would ruffle feathers in India, and they say that informally but that is probably one reason which keeps them from having more such institutes.

This is an impression and a more rigorous enquiry is needed if any serious conclusions are to be drawn from this.

Generous scholarships are being offered to South Asian students for studying Chinese language as well as other subjects in China. The China Scholarship Council has an MoU with Pakistan's Higher Education Commission which sends 1,000 college teachers and scientific researchers to reputed institutions for doctoral degrees in China. So, at any point in time there will be 1,000 people, i.e., if 100 graduate and come back then another 100 will go to China. In Sri Lanka, each year 23 Sri Lankans and a number of Maldivians have been awarded similar scholarships. Bangladesh and Nepal also send large numbers of students for higher studies to China. Relatively few Indian students have availed of these scholarship. However, more than 7,000 Indian students are pursuing courses in medicine and other disciplines of science and management in various universities at their own expense. Such factors indicate that China is gradually becoming an important destination for higher education.

According to many observers, China's soft power has obvious limitations. As long as China has many contentious issues to deal with, and as long as China is a one-party authoritarian system, it cannot compete either with the United States or even with India in terms of its soft power. As pointed out by John Lee (2010), 'While China's neighbours look at the country's rise with a mixture of apprehension and admiration, the story of India's re-emergence is more attractive to many States in the region. After all, unlike China, India has no history of aggression or domination in East or South East Asia. As the world's largest democracy with a vibrant press and a thriving entertainment industry, India has huge soft power advantages over China and its state controlled media. The implication is that India can take advantage of that good will as China's two giants battle for influence in the region and around the world.' Shashi Tharoor (2009) is often quoted in this context. He had said, 'In today's world it is not the size of the army that wins the war but the country that tells the better story.' Zhai Kun (2005) of the China Institutes of Contemporary International Relations (CICIR) writing on the subject agrees that 'China now has acquired some degree of soft power', but he asks whether this means that 'China has enough soft power.' An answer from a scholar from CICIR: 'No, it does not.

Aside from its economy and military, there are serious concerns on issues such as democracy and the Communist Party's anti-corruption campaign. These two issues, vital to China's image abroad are key components of soft power. A better image would make it easier for China to develop peacefully, while a bad image makes cooperation with other countries more difficult. A democratic or clean China may be preferable to a strong China.'

References

Kun, Zhai (2005). "China's Need for Soft Power", *IIAS Newsletter* 36, March. p.31, Available at *http://www.iias.nl/nl/36/IIAS_NL36_31.pdf*

Kurlantzick, Joshua(2007). *Charm Offensive: How China's Soft Power is Transforming the World*. New Haven: Yale University Press.

Lee, John (2010). "Unrealized Potential: India's Soft Power Ambitions in Asia", *CIS Foreign Policy Analysis* 4. June.

Palit, Paroma Sinha (2011). "Strategic Influence of Soft Power: Inferences for India from Chinese Engagement in south and South-East Asia", *ICRIER Policy Series*, August.

Pan, Esther (2006). "China's Soft Power Initiative", Backgrounder. Council for Foreign Relations Blog: Asia Unbound. *http://www.cfr.org/china/chinas-soft-power-initiative/p10715*

Tharoor, Shashi (2009). "Why Nations should Pursue Soft Power", *Youtube*. December 2.